MOORCROFT

The Phœnix Years

Moorcroft Pottery: Study in Nostalgia by Howard Phipps

Nostalgia in all its forms has to be kept in perspective and its best feature is to actually highlight the improvements which have taken place in our conditions of working and living. It is more than gratifying to see that the efforts of the last eighty years have been completed during the course of this year by the restructuring of the factory to a standard fit for the twenty-first century. Walter Moorcroft, December 1993

Fraser Street

MOORCROFT
The Phœnix
Years

WM PUBLICATIONS

First published in 1997 by W M Publications Limited
5 Town Street, Thaxted, Essex CM6 2LD
Distributed by W M Publications Limited
P.O. Box 2864, Ringwood, Hampshire BH24 3YE

Printed in Great Britain by Butler and Tanner, Frome and London

Design: Peter Campbell
Photographs: Gate Studios; E.L. Gibbs, Royal Borough of Windsor & Maidenhead;
Garry Leggett Studios; John Ross; Richard Blower

This book would not have been possible without the help of many
people. I must thank, in particular, Jo Rogers, Ann Geneva, Jean Brown, Alan Wright,
Judy Alexandria, Beverly Potts, Mr and Mrs WJS Moorcroft, Justin Emery, Talents of Windsor,
James MacIntyre & Co Ltd, Philip Allen, David Simmons and Kim Thompson,
and, most specially, my best friend, partner, collaborator,
critic, companion and wife, Maureen Edwards.
H.E.

The Moorcroft Pottery can be found in Cobridge
on Sandbach Road, Burslem, Stoke-on-Trent ST6 2DQ
Telephone: 01782 214 323 & 261 691 Facsimile: 01782 283 455

Contents

TO THE STAFF OF MOORCROFT POTTERY – WITH LOVE

Preface

The invitation to write the preface for *The Phoenix Years* has allowed me the long overdue opportunity to make a definitive statement for which I offer no excuses, and by the same token I do not seek pity: 'I'm a Potaholic'. What is more I know that I am not alone in enjoying this state of mind. My dear friend and Antiques Road Show colleague Henry Sandon 'came out' as a potaholic years ago and might possibly be regarded as one of the severest cases imaginable.

Unlike Henry, I have yet to feel the urge to share my bed with the odd pot, although my wife lives with the constant threat of opening her eyes one morning only to find a piece of Moorcroft pressed against her nose. Life without Moorcroft, for myself and thousands of others, is simply unthinkable and might be compared with the thought of life without the FA Cup Final or even worse, life without a baked jam roll.

Whilst writing *The Phoenix Years*, Hugh Edwards has well and truly put his cards on the table and can be recognised as a man who has gone past the point of no return – and I both salute him and embrace him as a kindred spirit.

Should you be considering adding this book to your collection on the understanding that it is a personal memoir offering yet another historical overview of Moorcroft, let me offer you this advice – gently close the book and place it back on the shelf. Hugh Edwards attempts and succeeds like no other writer before to offer the reader a rare insight into what I can only inadequately describe as the veritable soul of this much loved pottery.

The lively narrative leads chronologically through the many events of the past decade that have witnessed the pottery edge gently away from the abyss of potential bankruptcy to its present-day stance of being able to reclaim the title of being Britain's premier art pottery.

Hugh Edwards offers an honest and personal understanding of those events; his respect for his colleagues both past and present is unquestionable, whilst his enthusiasm and passion for Moorcroft Pottery is total.

His book made me smile. If you enjoy smiling, read on.

ERIC KNOWLES, FRSA

The Moorcroft stand at the British Empire Exhibition, Wembley 1924

William Moorcroft

Walter Moorcroft

John Moorcroft

A Brief History of Moorcroft Pottery

The founder of Moorcroft pottery William Moorcroft was born in 1872 in Burslem, Staffordshire, where the Works is still located today. His family was already linked to the Potteries, since his father Thomas was a well-known designer and china painter who specialised in floral decoration. When he was twelve, William attended classes in art and design at the Wedgwood Institute, which came to count him among their most distinguished graduates. By 1895 William was studying in South Kensington at what later became the Royal College of Art, gaining an Art Master's Certificate in 1897. Somewhat unusually, he also made close observations of the ancient and modern pottery and porcelain in the collections of the British Museum and the South Kensington Museum, a course he later pursued further in Paris.

William Moorcroft's career as a potter was launched when at the age of 24 he was offered a position as a designer with the china and earthenware manufacturers, James Macintyre & Company in Burslem. Since the 1830's, Macintyre's had made its name by manufacturing to a high standard a wide range of largely utilitarian commercial pottery and porcelain. They had diversified in 1893 into producing the ornamental art pottery made popular by William Morris and his followers. In March 1897 William Moorcroft took up his post, immediately designing new shapes and introducing an original highly stylised floral decoration which owed less to the Continental Art Nouveau style than it did to English designers. His new design was given the name Aurelian ware. Early in 1898, William became Manager of Ornamental Ware and developed a new range of decorative pottery using the techniques of slip-trailing and underglaze colour, which were to become his hallmarks. The result was called Florian ware, reflecting the floral basis of its motifs.

William Moorcroft drew his designs 'in the round', adapting them to fit every shape of pot, and controlled the execution of each piece of pottery in his department. Rare for a working potter and designer, William had also made a study of ceramic chemistry, which provided him with an understanding of the firm's laboratories, clayrooms and dipping house, as well as the commercial kilns in which the ware was fired. His knowledge of the entire spectrum of pottery design and manufacture enabled him to originate and supervise the whole range of ceramic production from initial concept and artistry through to the finished product – resulting in an artisanal philosophy which was to endure throughout his lifetime and which still continues to this day. These working methods contrasted with the majority of English art potters, who employed group practices.

Florian ware proved a great and immediate success, and within a year of being introduced was to be seen on sale at Liberty of London and Rouard of Paris, as well as Tiffany in New York. William won his first gold medal at the St. Louis International Exhibition of 1904, and other awards included a gold medal in Brussels in 1910 and a diploma of honour at Ghent in 1913. Indeed, during the period William worked for Macintyre it was his name rather than theirs which became an international byword, and this may ultimately have influenced their decision to cease making ornamental pottery.

Beginning in 1904 William's designs moved steadily away from Florian, starting with Flamminian ware whose warm luminous monochrome was reminiscent of oriental ceramics. The period between 1905 and 1911 saw a profusion of new patterns, including cornflower, pansy, wisteria and pomegranate. With these designs William embarked on a bolder style. At the same time he profitably supplied decorated ware for a growing number of silversmiths and platers to mount or set into stands. Most important was the close relationship established during this era with Liberty, who became William's most important client, also commissioning him to produce commemorative wares for the coronation of Edward VII in 1902 and for George V in 1911.

When in 1912 William Moorcroft was told Macintyre's were to close his department in June of the following year, it was to Liberty he turned for financial backing to build a new factory in which he could continue to produce his distinctive ornamental pottery. With Liberty providing two thirds and William one third of the backing, a new factory arose on the site of a former tile and brick company in Cobridge, where Moorcroft remains to this day. The same year of 1913 also saw William married to Florence Lovibond, a former Inspector of Factories for the Home Office. Between them, Florence and William supervised the construction of a simple, light, state-of-the-art workplace for their new company, Moorcroft Pottery, in contrast to the dangers and difficulties inherent in existing Victorian factories. It was the first modern factory building in the Potteries, and the first to function on one floor.

There William moved his team of 34 craftsmen and women, all of whom had worked with him at Macintyre's, and whose ware initially comprised the entire output of the new kiln. A 'bread and butter' line of pottery was needed for this new venture, with the result that one of Moorcroft's all-time successes, the Powder Blue tableware range produced in a wide variety of shapes and sizes at a reasonable price, came into being. Deemed by no less a critic than Nikolaus Pevsner 'undatedly perfect' in 1937, it remained in production until 1963. During the First World War conscription reduced the workforce, and along with other potters Moorcroft added government orders for beer and shaving mugs, hospital inhalers, and other basic domestic wares for the army to its production.

With the war's end Moorcroft pottery was able to expand, and throughout the 1920's and into the 30's successful trading continued, with the 20's especially enhancing the Company's international reputation. Export business flourished, particularly in Canada and Australia, but extending to South America, Scandinavia and elsewhere. This financial security allowed Moorcroft to concentrate on developing design and production, resulting in many notable new patterns. English flowers were still used, but strong natural designs based on fruit, exotic flowers and landscapes characterise this period. William's greatest technical achievement was to initiate the low temperature flambé glazes he was able to develop after building a special flambé kiln in 1919. Praised by the Japanese ambassador himself after seeing them displayed at an exhibition, these flambé pieces' secret firings were reputedly over- seen by William himself during long days and nights.

Central to Moorcroft's growing world-wide fashionability was the patronage extended by the Royal Family, especially Queen Mary. Beginning in 1913 when she admired some Florian ware during a visit to the Potteries and culminating in a visit to Moorcroft's stunning exhibition stand at the famous British Empire Exhibition at Wembley in 1924, the Queen publicly demonstrated her approval of Moorcroft pottery by purchasing pieces regularly. In 1928, the Company was granted a Royal Warrant and appointed Potters to Her Majesty the Queen, an honour she reaffirmed after William's death when his son, Walter, took charge of the Company.

The world-wide depression of the 1930s was a difficult period for Moorcroft, as for all pottery manufacturers, and export sales constituted a large portion of turnover. To survive in the home market Moorcroft produced very diverse ranges, including even such items as named children's mugs and glazes to match particular fabrics fashionable at the time. Styles were changing as well, and Moorcroft responded with simplified designs and more abstract patterns, sometimes incorporating Art Deco borders for good measure, as well as redrawing earlier designs in newer modes. Moorcroft pottery continued to be honoured with awards and was featured at the Royal Academy Exhibition in 1935 and the World's Fair in New York in 1938.

During the Second World War diversity of production was maintained, with the addition of an elegant undecorated Austerity tableware. The war years proved a time of struggle, and only William's strong will ensured the survival both of himself and his Pottery. Throughout his entire career, he never employed a manager or another designer, insisting on responsibility for every aspect of production. In 1945 William was taken ill, surviving only long enough for his elder son Walter to arrive home on compassionate leave from the army. By the time of his death, many examples of William Moorcroft's work had been acquired by museums in the United States, Canada, Germany, and Italy, as well as in the United Kingdom. In 1972 the Victoria and Albert Museum mounted a retrospective centenary exhibition of his work.

Walter, who inherited his father's artistic flair, had begun working with him in 1935 directly from school. William passed on to Walter not only his working methods, but also insights into every aspect of pottery design and manufacture – including his fiercely guarded flambé methods. After assuming command of the company in 1945 Walter was soon creating designs in his own style, which he had begun doing in the late 1930's, and sustained the company's reputation until his retirement in 1987. John Moorcroft, William's younger son from his second marriage to Hazel Lasenby of the Liberty family, joined the company in 1962 with special responsibility for sales and marketing. He became managing director in 1984.

William Moorcroft once styled himself as 'Potter, Chemist, Designer, Managing Director, Secretary' – a combination no one person could any longer embody. Yet a newspaper article entitled 'A Potter of Genius' commenting on the 1924 Moorcroft display at Wembley has proved prophetic, summarising as it does the achievement of Moorcroft's continuing distinctive quality: 'Moorcroft pottery will be the quest of collectors of future generations, for it is the perfect expression of the potter's art. In design, harmony, delicacy and richness of colouring this stands unique among ceramic ware of today.'

ANN GENEVA

Mosaic of pre-war Moorcroft shards taken from a tip at the rear of the Works. Designed and made by the American artist, Candace Bahouth, the mosaic was unveiled by the late Arnold Mountford in 1991 and hangs on the wall of the Moorcroft factory shop.

ONE

Last Rites

The ponderous litany of the lawyers seemed endless and dull. Hugh Edwards and Richard Dennis were watching a corporate completion meeting. Hugh had attended many in his life as a commercial lawyer, but never had he been so impatient for the tedious formalities to come to an end. For the first time he was the client – and he hated it. After eighty-nine glorious years of contribution to the applied arts there was a risk that Moorcroft Pottery might pass into history like all its predecessors. To acquire control of a company as Edwards and Dennis were about to do is something that rarely happens to most people. To acquire control of a once-famous art pottery was a unique experience. Completion of the share purchase was seeming just about as elusive as finding an example of William Moorcroft's old Florian Ship vase, photographed at the end of the last century, but never found to this day.

If Edwards was impatient, Richard Dennis was unquestionably bored by the whole proceedings. Warranties, financial assistance problems, debentures and share transfers were passing right over the top of his head, as they would most sane people. If Edwards signed, Richard signed; if Edwards said yes, Richard said yes – and still the lawyers could not agree. John Moorcroft had lawyers. The current owners, the Ropers, had lawyers. Hugh and Richard had a lawyer. There were lawyers everywhere, and none of them agreed. Nor was there any sign they would ever agree. The situation had developed into a three-sided tug of war and was in danger of becoming an all-night macho session, much loved by lawyers who could continue to charge fees, possibly at premium rates.

After a final frustrated glance at Richard, who looked as if he were about to fall asleep, Edwards decided to act. Warranties, he said crossly to the lawyers, were

FACING: *Pot (c. 1914) found lying in pieces in a cellar boiler-room and partially restored for the Moorcroft Museum: Height 14"*

*Mini-boxes and small vases,
produced from 1980–86*

meaningless when those warranties were to be given by a very old friend. The subject of that particular comment was John Moorcroft, younger son of William Moorcroft, the founding father of Moorcroft Pottery.

The paperwork would be signed as it was, Edwards told the startled lawyers, and completion of the share acquisition had to take place within the hour. John, who had been uncertain about the drift of the meeting generally, looked relieved. Richard Dennis shuffled slightly in his chair to indicate his approval and the collection of lawyers stopped their money clocks ticking. David Boutcher, Edwards' colleague at his City of London law firm Richards Butler, had represented Hugh and Richard in their acquisition of seventy per cent of the shares of Moorcroft Pottery from the present owners, Michael, Andrew and Steven Roper. Boutcher had watched the almost surreal process by which Edwards mutated from professional adviser to client with dry amusement, tinged with unease. The world of commerce and industry was littered with lawyers who had crossed the line, abandoning their legal training and a comfortable life in the law in a genuine belief that management would provide a more fulfilling career. Belief and reality sometimes live uncomfortably together. In committing himself to Moorcroft without simultaneously detaching himself from Richards Butler, Edwards had taken a significant risk – and Boutcher knew it. What Boutcher could not have known was the turmoil of conflicting thoughts churning away in Edwards' mind, out of which eventually came a stubborn and unshakeable belief that with Richard Dennis at his elbow he could pull Moorcroft through while remaining totally loyal to his partners in the law firm.

The sixteenth of September 1986 was to become a date indelibly imprinted on Edwards' mind. In the ordinary course of his work as a commercial lawyer, he had experienced commercial decline before. Even so, Edwards had not adequately braced himself for the emotional shock he had received as he drove his car through the old iron gates into the Moorcroft car park. In the late afternoon light of that early autumn day, Moorcroft's magnificent bottle kiln seemed to soar majestically into the sky. The great structure stood proud and unbending with a will and a strength all its own.

Those staff still remaining at Moorcroft were all waiting in the decorating shop. There were no smiles, no idle chatter; only the vacant look of ordinary people who were not sure where to go and faced the prospect of being unable to pay their rent or mortgage from that day, unless 'Mr John' succeeded in finding a suitable buyer. A sharp rain shower a few minutes earlier had caused the holes in the roof to leak, and water was plopping rhythmically into strategically placed plastic buckets on the floor. Earlier that week a brick from the rim of the bottle kiln itself had crashed through the roof of the factory shop, narrowly missing one of Moorcroft's loyal customers in its downward path. The ancient electric kilns, installed in the late 1950's to replace the original coal-fired bottle kilns, were rusty, and part of the external casing on the biscuit kiln was actually peeling off. As a result, each firing cycle in these 'old bangers', as John Moorcroft called them, took twenty-seven hours.

Edwards' eyes swept over pile upon pile of ceramic mini-boxes and small vases with their moulded designs, which included Campanula and Geranium introduced by Moorcroft in 1984. It was as if the collapse in the size of the company's bank balance had provoked a parallel collapse in the size of the pots on offer. Most of the graceful old Moorcroft shapes had gone in the drive to take the company into the mass market. The enormity of the task ahead was as stark as the decay and the despair.

David Boutcher set off to Derby to see his parents on his way back to London. After the lawyer had gone, John stood with his staff; like them, he was uncertain what to say. To break an awkward silence, Hugh and Richard outlined the ideas they had in mind. Perhaps the Moorcroft staff had reached that level of despair which only the near-jobless can understand. Perhaps they simply did not believe what they heard. Perhaps it had all been said two years earlier, when the Moorcroft family had sold their shares to the Roper brothers. John had not sold. He had held on to his inheritance. Whatever the reason, the sea of faces remained stoic and unmoved. At first Edwards felt rejected, but on reflection it had probably not been reasonable to

Moulded designs. Campanula and Geranium, 1984-6

expect praise simply for buying the company. Praise had to be earned by success. Laughter and happiness at work were human reactions which fed on success and the security that goes with it.

After the last employee had left for the day, Hugh explained to John the detailed timetable of the Edwards/Dennis five-year recovery plan. John was an important part of that plan. When everything was collapsing around him, John had not given up his personal fight for the company which carried his family name. For John, it was not just his job that was at risk. It was a loss of pride and esteem; it was the loss of a once great name in the Potteries, and the loss of the last surviving independent art pottery in Europe with a once great reputation.

It was John who had contacted Hugh in London to discuss a possible purchase of the Roper shares in Moorcroft as an alternative to a sale of the Moorcroft name. Production at Cobridge might have ceased, the company liquidated and the site sold for possible development. For John that would have spelt the end of the business as he knew it. He already knew that Hugh and Richard were working together on the first definitive book on Moorcroft Pottery, scheduled for publication in 1987. Additionally, he knew that Hugh counted among his major clients one of the biggest companies operating in the Potteries. Indeed, John's instincts told him that Hugh was something more than a commercial lawyer and business man: in Edwards he had a personal friend who knew and understood the ceramics industry, as well as how to arrange and manage its finance. Above all, Hugh knew and understood Moorcroft pottery as an almost life-long collector. John Moorcroft had all of this in mind when he made his fateful phone call to Edwards at Richards Butler in the early summer of 1986.

The lawyer's initial reaction had been to pass off the problem John had presented by contacting other major players in the ceramics industry, including his own clients. It had almost worked. However, by September all his potential purchasers had declared a lack of interest. In corporate language, that meant Moorcroft as Edwards knew it was all but dead. The only remaining option open to Edwards was to act himself, or watch a wonderful old company put its trust in fate. He was not a particularly wealthy man, and it was his wife, Maureen, who pointed out that at the end of the day their collection of old Moorcroft, built up over twenty years of married life, could be sold if the Moorcroft venture turned out to be a total disaster.

After a sleepless night drinking tea together, Maureen offered to mortgage her office premises to raise money, and the two of them decided to stake their prized collection of old Moorcroft pottery. Hugh then telephoned Richard Dennis early the following morning. He had three reasons for doing so. The first was the work they had done together on the Moorcroft pottery book. The second was Edwards' confidence in the instinctive skill Richard possessed in appraising the quality of art pottery, literally with the tips of his fingers; and the third was that Richard's wife, Sally, had been an eminent fashion designer under her maiden name, Tuffin.

Sally had trained at the Walthamstow School of Art and later in the Fashion School of the Royal College of Art. With an RCA Silver Medal to complement her Des.R.C.A., she went on to develop an international reputation during the 1960's and into the 1970's as a fashion designer in her firm Foale and Tuffin. There was just an outside chance that Sally might agree to take on the role of Design Director at Moorcroft. Twenty-four hours later, the Dennises agreed to join the Edwards in a unique partnership which was to last for six years.

The original five-year recovery plan was relatively simple. The Edwards would take control of all commercial and financial matters; John would act as ambassador for his family name and promote Moorcroft Pottery worldwide; while Richard and Sally would take charge of design. A Collectors' Club would be formed without delay, and a Museum created as soon as possible. Other innovations and improvements would follow in accordance with a strict timetable, finances permitting. Indeed the list of objectives Hugh and Richard drew up in the small flat above Richard's shop in Kensington Church Street boasted no fewer than twenty-nine items! It was in the area of sales that one of the biggest question marks remained, and, as Richard Dennis remarked, a small miracle was required if Moorcroft sales were to be restored to their levels in the company's heyday during the mid-1920's.

Those early weeks at Moorcroft were exhausting both for Richard who lived in Somerset and for Edwards who lived in Essex. On Friday evening, at the end of a full and demanding week at his law practice in the City, Edwards would drive the one hundred and seventy-five miles to Stoke-on-Trent, often returning home late Sunday evening. As a ceramics dealer Richard had been permanently 'on the road', but a weekly and sometimes twice-weekly visit to Stoke-on-Trent added at least another five hundred miles to his already gruelling schedule. Even so, within three weeks of completion of the share purchase Maureen's office had been mortgaged, and National Westminster Bank had agreed Edwards' financial plan to rescue the company without a single personal guarantee.

*Trevor Critchlow,
mould-maker*

Both Hugh and Richard had been seriously upset by the loss of old Moorcroft shapes so sought after by collectors. Since the end of the last century, Moorcroft shapes had been famous for their elegance, and to start the process of repairing the damage Richard called upon the services of Roger Michell. Roger sat with his potter's wheel for a week in the Works, producing shape after shape in raw wet clay for mould-maker, Trevor Critchlow, to model. From his wheel came Moorcroft's massive 27″ RM3 vase and many others – some practical, some not; some elegant, some not. It was a start, and his work brought with it a new vision of shapes to come as well as being a meaningful step towards the restoration of professional pride for a demoralised workforce, who now had something new and substantial to challenge their skills.

While Roger offered new inspiration to uplift and broaden Moorcroft's concept of shape, Richard set about methodically collecting together a variety of old Moorcroft pots which lay neglected and forgotten around the Works. Some stood under work benches gathering dust, some were used as doorstops or as decorator's bowls, and some perched precariously on the top of the old oak cabinets made by Liberty in the 1920's. These cabinets themselves stood sad and dilapidated against the damp brick walls of the Works, their woodwork almost grey with dirt and dust. In the cellar, their contents buried under six inches of sulphur-ridden soot, Hugh and Richard found a large number of old tea chests stacked up to the ceiling. Some were so old that the wooden veneer had split open exposing the brittle yellow tissue paper inside. Richard, the ceramics dealer, had been excited by the discovery. So was Edwards, the collector. In the chests were old Moorcroft pots, some dating back to the First World War. All were still wrapped in their original tissue paper, now old and dry and so impregnated with sulphur that it crumbled into fragments when handled.

Unpacking those battered boxes with their seal of soot was one of the dirtiest and yet one of the most exciting jobs that Richard and Hugh had ever undertaken. Literally before their eyes there appeared not only the means to generate a stream of cash in the factory shop over the critical months ahead, but also a solid foundation for the Moorcroft Museum. It was a stroke of good fortune which boosted morale and gave an unexpected impetus to Moorcroft's financial recovery.

The Moorcroft sales profile was a nightmare. The Factory Shop, which Gill

FACING: *Shapes thrown by Roger Michell: Autumn 1986*

Moorcroft, John's wife, had managed since 1971, had shown a mixture of static or falling sales throughout the decade. One reason may have been that Moorcroft designs had not changed materially for ten years or more and were often described coldly and rather unfairly by prima donnas in the English antiques trade as 'dated and stale'. The Roper brothers' plan had been to reduce the cost and quality of Moorcroft to make it available to a wider but less sophisticated mass market. Edwards is the first to acknowledge that as a plan it was commercially justified, even though in the case of Moorcroft it failed. Campanula and Geranium, simple and uninspired moulded designs introduced between 1984 and 1986, invariably made Edwards shudder whenever he saw them – particularly the mini-boxes. He was later to learn that his dislike was shared by Walter Moorcroft who had been asked to create the designs in the first place!

Walter's role at Moorcroft was less than clear. The deal negotiated with the Roper brothers was that he should retire in 1987 on a modest pension which Moorcroft would pay. The pension prospect faded dramatically with the company's possible collapse, but re-emerged with the arrival of Hugh and Richard. In 1986, at almost seventy years of age, Walter Moorcroft could look back on a career in his family business which had started in 1935. Walter's father, William, had been responsible for producing Moorcroft pottery since 1897 – ending only with his death in 1945. Walter then took immediate control, after six years military service in the army, and had remained in charge at the Works until the arrival of the Roper brothers in 1984.

His half-brother, John, joined the company in 1962. John is the first to admit that he was born when his father was sixty-six years old. William Moorcroft's first wife, Florence, had two children, Walter and his elder sister, Beatrice. After Florence's death in 1926, William married Hazel Lasenby, a member of the Liberty family. John Moorcroft was born in 1938, and his father, William, died only seven years later. Nowadays, John and Walter show every sign that they regard each other as old friends as well as brothers, and the relationship has endured well over the years.

If grim sales statistics were needed, Hugh and Richard had only to look at the Greater London postal area where receipts had fallen to just £2,400 in the previous year. Even Liberty, with their family ties, had shown Moorcroft the door, ending a traditional relationship which dated to the early years of the century. Export sales,

FACING: *Old Moorcroft pieces found lying around the Works and now in the Moorcroft museum*

so strong after the Second World War, had collapsed – the North American continent was little more than a sales desert. New designs and financial control could be only partial solutions to Moorcroft's problems. Edwards worried continuously about sales, but until the question of new designs had been resolved the sales drive could not begin. To keep sales moving and to promote exports, Richard Dennis made contact with an old Canadian friend, David Simmons, hoping to persuade him to take on a Moorcroft distributorship in Canada. It was a long shot, but it hit the target. Simmonds agreed to Richard's proposition, against the promise of a special limited edition vase and a modest re-working of one or two of Walter Moorcroft's more recent designs. That simple arrangement gave Moorcroft a strong sales outlet in Canada. In return, Canada received Sally's famous limited edition Polar Bear vase, so sought after in the secondary market today.

As soon as she joined the company, Sally Dennis quickly acquainted herself with the finer details involved in the technique of making Moorcroft's unique style of art pottery. Moorcroft is the only significant pottery in Europe where the decoration is applied to the raw clay before firing. The first stage of decoration, after the 'green' or unfired pot has been turned on the lathe to perfect its shape, is to transfer the design from a piece of tracing paper onto the pot through the medium of a special purple ink. With the ink outline safely on the clay, the piece is ready for the Moorcroft tube-liners to start their work. Tube-liners are rare and highly skilled artists who use a fine pipette with a 'squeeze bag' affixed to it which the tube-liners fill with liquid clay or 'slip'. By gently squeezing the bag, the tube-liners force an extrusion of slip to flow out of a small hole at the end of the pipette. Then, with a skill which involves consummate manual dexterity, the slip 'trails' (i.e., follows) the purple design lines which have been put in place on the surface of the pot. Once the tube-liners have completed their work, the unfired, wet pot is put in a heated drying room for the excess moisture to evaporate. Only when it has thoroughly dried out is the pot then ready for the Moorcroft decorators to apply their own special art.

The colour pigments used by Moorcroft decorators are metallic oxides in powder form. The colour is carefully mixed with water and then 'floated' onto the pot with fine, soft paint brushes. The Moorcroft decorating technique is very much a process of 'building' colours, one on top of the other, until the desired result has been achieved. By floating on the colours, the water passes from the hairs of the

FACING: *The process of making a Moorcroft pot: Turning, tubelining, painting and dipping*

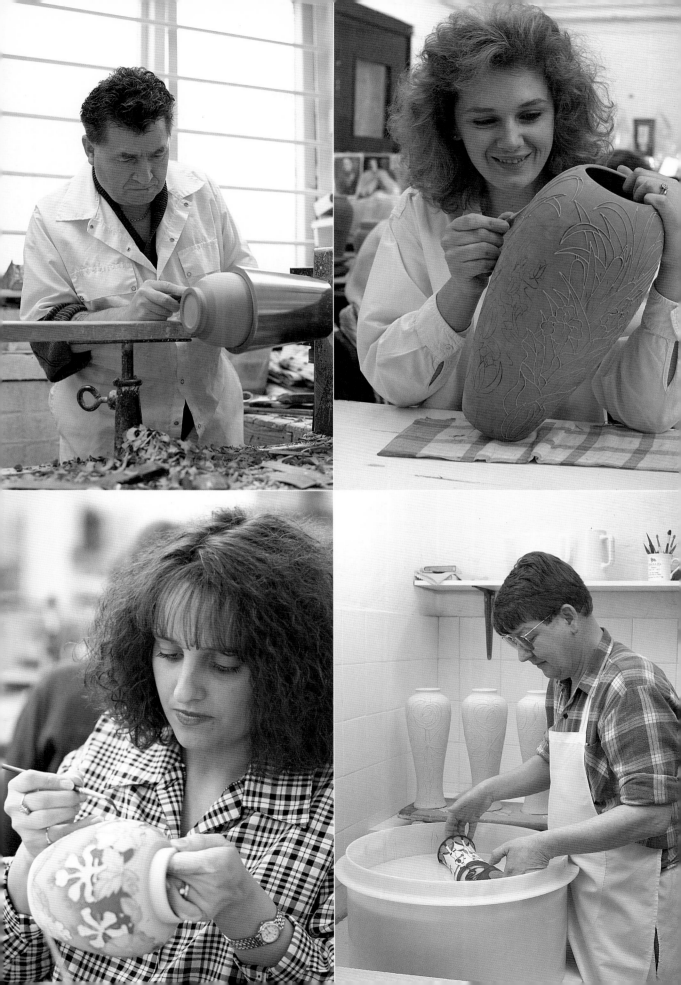

brush, still impregnated with colour, on to the surface of the pot where it is absorbed into the dry clay body leaving the colour behind. The immediate effect achieved by applying colour in this way is similar to the negative of a colour photograph, and it is only after the first or 'biscuit' firing that the real colours can be seen. Biscuit firing takes place at temperatures in excess of 1,100° centigrade. Then after cooling the pot is dipped in a special liquid glaze before its second firing, known in the ceramics industry as the 'glost' firing. When the pot emerges from the glost kiln, it can be seen in all its final glory with that very special richness, depth and brilliance of colour which have become the hallmarks of Moorcroft pottery.

Anemone vases after biscuit-firing

When he first called the Dennises to ask them to join the team, Edwards knew that Sally, with her husband Richard, had launched the Dennis Chinaworks from their home in Somerset a year or so earlier. Indeed, any special aspects of making Moorcroft pottery with which Sally had been unfamiliar before the Dennises acquired their shares would have been well and truly learned by the middle of October 1986. The potential problem which caused Edwards growing concern was the design direction in which Sally appeared to be moving, rather than her ability to master the Moorcroft medium. He started to worry when he saw her concentrating on a round pot onto which she had worked a clever design which used the word 'Moorcroft'. As salesman Steven Swann somewhat unkindly remarked at the time, there would be little sales demand for a pot featuring a name which most retailers had forgotten.

Soon after they took control of Moorcroft, the new owners initiated a competition among the staff to see if there was any latent design talent which might be tapped. The results of the competition were encouraging. A dragon decorated in green and yellow had been designed by Moorcroft's mould-maker, Trevor Critchlow. The original piece had been quickly followed by a variation on the theme, featuring a traditional blue and purple dragon on a dark blue ground. Marjorie Kubanda, a former paintress who acted as Moorcroft's biscuit ware selector, had produced a fruit and vine design drawn on a planter, while two paintresses, Wendy

FACING: *Pieces found in the cellar tea chests now in the Moorcroft museum. Tallest vase 12″*

Mason and Julie Dolan, produced some deceptively simple ivory pieces decorated with ivy.

This activity, combined with a genuine desire to help, galvanised Walter Moorcroft himself into action. The result was a pair of new designs from Walter, using chestnut leaves and a pineapple plant. When it came to the crunch, the new owners became uneasy at the prospect of putting staff designs into production. From the outset, Ivy proved difficult and Richard's initial words of caution on the subject were borne out. Edwards had tried to keep an open mind, but it was his underlying unease at the apparent lack of urgency in mainstream design which had encouraged him to agree to producing a few staff pieces. Shortly after the Works' design competition, the Dennises announced they were making efforts themselves to prepare a special range for Moorcroft's Australian distributor, Philip Allen. Another sideshow, Edwards remarked crossly and a little unfairly to John at the time. The result was Banksia, a flower design which used a mix of green and grey colours. Of design work for a new mainstream range for 1987, there was little evidence.

Towards the end of November, and by then seriously perturbed, Edwards had called round to see Richard in his London shop. Sally was reported to be working on two designs, Violet and Rose. The style, Richard had announced cautiously, would be 'different'. Edwards could say little, understood less, and decided to accept the word 'different' at face value. In so doing, Moorcroft became committed to Sally's very personal approach to design. Edwards was not to know it at the time, but eleven years later, during Moorcroft's centenary year in 1997, Sally's geometric Violet range with modified colours would still be in production.

The primary importance of both Violet and Rose was that they broke down a traditional Moorcroft concept of design style, and in so doing introduced a wider spectrum of customers to Moorcroft pottery. Something more than traditional design values had to be identified and created to steer the company away from the abyss of commercial oblivion. Edwards was delighted at what he had seen and heard, and he relaxed visibly.

Violet and Rose apart*, to survive beyond 1987 still more new designs had to explode from Moorcroft as they had never done before. Edwards, the Moorcroft collector, was not prepared to rely merely on Banksia or a geometric Violet and Rose on their own. Neither was he particularly happy at the prospect of little more

---

* All designs referred to in this paragraph are featured in colour in the book *Moorcroft* (Revised Edition 1897/1993) by Paul Atterbury, published by Dennis and Edwards

than slight variables of Walter Moorcroft's designs or the unproven offerings from Moorcroft staff. After discussion with Richard, Hugh approached Philip Richardson, art master at Friends' School, Saffron Walden – the same school where Sally herself had been educated. Before the Christmas break, designs by Philip Richardson called Honeycomb, Reeds at Sunset and Fairy Rings were all approved as new ranges for 1987.

Simultaneously, a decision was taken to run Sally's Banksia, Violet and Rose designs as full ranges. Walter's Pineapple Plant and Chestnut Leaf pieces would be produced as limited editions. For good measure, and to encourage Moorcroft staff to play a full part in their own destiny, Dragon by Trevor Critchlow was introduced as a small range in both its colourways, while Marjorie Kubanda's Fruit and Vine planter featured as a limited edition. Designs by Walter using Tulip, Maize and Arum Lily were also made available as limited editions to fulfil some of the promises made to Moorcroft's new Canadian distributor, David Simmons. With what could only be described as a medley of assorted designs, Moorcroft was ready for both the January Light Show at Olympia, London, and the International Spring Fair at the National Exhibition Centre, Birmingham, which opened at the beginning of February.

Treasure trove buried in soot

TWO

Miracles at Bethlehem and Birmingham

Alan Wright was unique, a master salesman with a successful career already be-hind him as a giftware retailer at the quality end of the market. After disposing of his retail business, Alan's reward for success was a continuous queue of manu-facturers all keen to employ him on a hefty commission of ten per cent. In January 1987, with his wife Rene, Alan had decided to take a winter break in Israel and make a tour of the Holy Land. Quite independently, and before their involvement in Moorcroft, Hugh and his wife Maureen had also decided to make a personal pilgrimage to the Holy Land, accompanied by their Parish Priest, Dr Tim Fawcett and his wife Jo. The frenzied design and trial activity at Moorcroft before Christ-mas in preparation for the 1987 Light Show at Olympia and the International Spring Fair at Birmingham's National Exhibition Centre had almost persuaded the Edwards to cancel their holiday. It had been Richard Dennis who insisted that the two of them continue with their plans, and with feelings of genuine relief Hugh and Maureen arrived in Jerusalem with their guests.

It was several days before the Edwards introduced themselves to fellow tour members, Alan and Rene, and a further two days before Hugh and Alan confided in the other details of their respective professions. Alan, it seemed, concentrated his freelance sales work in Greater London, in which he had his major retail con-tacts. Although he kept his thoughts to himself, Edwards calculated that if Alan took ten per cent of gross sales as commission, all that he had to offer him was the princely income of £240 per annum. For his part, Alan unwittingly rubbed salt into the wound by telling Edwards that he had only recently turned down an account which would have yielded more than £10,000 per annum on the same basis!

Years later, Edwards would recall that if a miracle was to happen, Bethlehem

FACING: *Above: left, Philip Allen; right, Steven Swann, Moorcroft sales manager with Debbie Edwards of the Leeds retailer James Macintyre.* BELOW: *left, David Simmons (with Canadian Polar Bear vase); right, Gill Moorcroft, secre-tary of the Moorcroft Collectors' Club*

Alan Wright at Liberty with buyer, Julia Marsh

was probably the appropriate location. Towards the end of their visit to the holy places of the Christian religion, Hugh and Alan were sitting together on a roughly hewn lump of subterranean rock, said to be the 'manger' of biblical fame. Both were waiting for their respective wives to catch them up, and in a matter of minutes Edwards rapidly sketched to Alan an outline of the Moorcroft story; his own career; his recent involvement with Moorcroft; the present disastrous sales position; details of the new designs; the two imminent trade fairs, and his own passionate wish to ensure the survival of an art pottery already eighty-nine years old. Alan looked at Edwards carefully, weighing up both the apprehension in his face and the reasons for his original decision to become involved in Moorcroft. Holidays should not be mixed with business. Alan was very clear about that, but he promised to seek out Edwards at the Birmingham Spring Fair the following month.

For some years falling sales at trade shows had made them occasions of increasing unease at Moorcroft, and for John Moorcroft the opening of the 1987 Birmingham Spring Fair was a tense moment as a result. If the designs by his new colleagues failed, Hugh would lose his Moorcroft pottery collection and Maureen her office; Richard would lose money; but John would lose everything. There had already been encouraging signs, and indeed some limited success at the Olympia Light Show the preceding month. Sally's Violets on a Roger Michell lamp base had caught the eye of the Liberty lighting buyer, and Liberty had reopened their Moorcroft account as a result. Orders had generally been higher than expected, and for John the Birmingham Fair opened with a mix of apprehension and optimism.

Sunday, traditionally a good day for orders from small family businesses, had seen sales move forward sharply from levels gleaned from Moorcroft's sketchy and rather sad records for the preceding year – but there was no sign of Alan Wright. The following day, however, just as he was about to lose hope, Edwards found himself staring at the grey-haired man himself, who appeared on the Moorcroft stand as if from nowhere. Alan was looking carefully at each piece on display, and for some reason Edwards suddenly felt self-conscious about the tatty trade stand fixtures which only a few days earlier had doubled as an 'office' at the

Works, and which had been 'freshened' for Birmingham by nothing more than a lick of olive green paint.

Only a few questions were asked, and, yes, Edwards told him, sales in the London area would produce an initial commission of £240 per annum. Alan smiled and walked away. Edwards' heart sank. So much for dreams! Perhaps he and Richard were nothing more than a pair of amateur optimists, doomed to be casualties in the world of industry and applied arts. An hour later Alan returned accompanied by the Selfridges' buyer. Edwards took the offered hand and shook it, uncertain whether to laugh or cry. To this day, that handshake is the only contract Alan has ever received. But within twelve months, twenty per cent of Moorcroft's sales were coming from the London postal area. The Moorcroft miracle had happened. Alan would spearhead a sales drive in that most important of all markets, London itself, and in him Moorcroft had acquired one of the finest and most experienced quality salesmen operating in Britain.

Midway through 1987, with a strong pattern of increased orders already on the books, Richard and Sally had taken the Edwards out to dinner at a favoured Italian restaurant near their shop. Hugh sensed trouble in the air, and waited for the storm to break. The Dennises were awkward and tense. It was not the Moorcroft finances. Those had been improving steadily. Good pricing and a good order book were both in place. It was not the sales drive. The arrival of Alan Wright had seen to that. Plans for the Moorcroft Museum were moving forward, and Richard, on his own estimate, was hopeful that it would open sometime in 1989. It had already been decided that some of the pieces found in the cellars and around the Works would form the basis of the Museum collection, supplemented by discrete purchases, as well as the loan of pots from the directors' personal collections. The display would be housed in the refurbished oak cabinets made by Liberty for Moorcroft for use at the British Empire Exhibition, Wembley in 1924.

The Collectors' Club had also been launched in accordance with the five-year plan, and Gill Moorcroft herself had been appointed Club Secretary. Both Hugh and Richard were reluctant to contain Gill's talents within the narrow confines of the Factory Shop, and to encourage her to move she was offered a Moorcroft directorship. Her simple choice was either to take on the Club responsibilities as a Director or stay where she was. Gill's decision marked the beginning of that great network of friends with a common cause which is now the 5,000 strong Moorcroft Collectors' Club.

Before the main course arrived, the Dennises mentioned the reason for their concern. The original agreement had been that the two of them would control design, with Sally as Design Director. In the event, 1987 had arrived with offerings from Walter Moorcroft, Philip Richardson, and the staff, as well as Sally. This was not what had been agreed, and Philip Richardson's continued involvement in the design process was clearly not welcome. Hugh was worried in case Philp Richardson would feel used and then abused for the work he had already done, and for which no payment had been offered or expected. An attempt to further involve him in a 1988 limited edition fell on deaf ears.

The Dennises were right, of course. The original plans for design included Director responsibilities for Sally. The Dennises had given Edwards a free hand in financial control and had supported all his decisions. There was no alternative but to confirm their analysis. Even so, Edwards felt that it was necessary to repeat the totality of the deal. Designs had to be delivered in time for photography each year. New designs had to be commercial and capable of production by the Moorcroft workforce, and above all designs had to be of the highest quality. Sally's training and experience uniquely qualified her for the role of design director and this was why Edwards had invited the Dennises to join the team in the first place.

Despite these qualifications, Edwards felt ill at ease. If this all-powerful design duo were ever to leave, the potential harm to Moorcroft and its unique workforce would be serious. All his life Edwards had sought to avoid reliance on others. Nevertheless, in the case of Moorcroft, he had agreed to the Dennises' control of design at the outset in the same way that commercial responsibility rested solely with him. Deep inside him lurked disappointment that staff were unlikely to be asked again to initiate designs. Apart from that there was nothing else to discuss. The Dennises had correctly re-stated the original deal.

Moorcroft's vulnerability was a line of thought which continued to exercise Hugh's mind for some months. While Richard channelled his energy into the finishing touches of the Moorcroft Museum, Hugh, urged on by his wife, was left to contemplate more mundane problems – including the Moorcroft toilets and washing facilities. The men's urinal was open to the stars, and in high summer the walls had a habit of turning a nasty shade of green. The smell was often dreadful. The 'ladies', although covered, boasted hand-painted wash basins installed in 1913. The men had no hot water; in the ladies hot water was intermittent. As soon as funds permitted, the first task to be completed was the repair and restoration of Moorcroft's historic bottle kiln. While toilets might smell, falling bricks could kill. That fact alone dictated priorities. Eventually Moorcroft secured a National

Heritage Award for the high standard of its restoration work of the bottle kiln, now as then a Grade II listed building.

A large heap of ash, clinker and shards dumped at the rear of the Works dated back to the early 1920's. From the top of the heap grew a pussy willow, much loved by Hugh and much hated by Richard, whose dealer's instincts encouraged him to request that the heap be broken up, sifted and searched. Moorcroft had urgent need of additional car-parking space, and as a result Richard won. With Moor-croft's directors moving behind the digger with baskets and boxes, the greatest-ever collection of old Moorcroft shards was put together over a period of two days. In Richard's mind a grand strategy had formed. The shards of pottery were all packed off to the world-famous American artist, Candace Bahouth, who turned them into a stunning and unique mosaic of the Moorcroft factory itself, a mosaic which now has pride of place on a wall in the Factory Shop. On 15 June 1991, the mosaic was unveiled, to the joy of all those concerned, by Arnold Mountford CBE, a well-known figure in the Potteries. Sadly, he died shortly afterwards, and in some sense the great mosaic stands as a tribute to his life's work in creating Stoke-on-Trent's own world-famous City Museum and Art Gallery.

Damp walls do not make for a healthy work place. As soon as sufficient funds had been realised from the sale of what was to become known as the 'cellar stock', the brick fabric of the factory was sandblasted externally, rotten cement infill re-moved, and the walls re-pointed, sealed and painted. In parallel, towards the end of 1989, an ambitious scheme was initiated to replace the rotten and leaking roof of the Works over a period of six years. New electric kilns were installed, cutting down the total firing cycle from twenty-seven hours to fifteen. Edwards was par-ticularly proud of the new kilns. Their method of construction not only conserved heat but also recycled it throughout the firing cycle. Small computers controlled temperatures to the exact level required for a particular truck or size of pottery, something William Moorcroft had to worry about throughout a firing cycle lasting three days in the coal-fired bottle kilns many decades earlier.

The cost of modernising the Works was enormous, and it was not until 1990 that either the Dennises or the Edwards felt able to take any form of remuneration whatever for their efforts. Richard guided and encouraged his wife through her new design presentations as they matured, and by 1992 Sally Tuffin had designed no fewer than eighteen new ranges: one with four colour variables and one with two, as well as forty-nine limited or special editions of one kind or another and six year plates. As if this prodigious output was not enough, there were also a number of special pieces designed for in-store promotions and special events including the popular Collectors' Club Open Weekends, the first of which was held in June 1988.

With new ranges and special editions regularly available, the sales team, inspired by Alan Wright, produced a pattern of sales growth that would have made any ceramics manufacturer green with envy. Put simply, Alan Wright and Steven Swann now had something to sell, a story to tell, and enthusiasm nurtured by success. At Hugh's suggestion, Alan had taken over the whole of the south of England in addition to London, leaving Steven the north of England, Scotland and Wales. The line between the two had been fairly drawn, and Steven began to polish and refine his own art of selling from the style and experience of his senior colleague. At his request, Alan was also given the task of promoting sales in the United States, a request with which the Moorcroft Board was very happy to agree.

Between them, John Moorcroft and Alan Wright instituted a sales revolution. Alan set out to organise the first of three visits which the company made to the huge New York Gift Fair using his contacts with the Westminster Chamber of Commerce, who at that time were sponsoring companies attempting to break into new export markets. John took steps to consolidate Moorcroft's ties with its Australian distributor, Philip Allen, who had become involved shortly before the arrival of Hugh and Richard in 1986. David Simmons in Canada moved into the local trade show circuits and within two years Moorcroft was exhibiting regularly in the United States, Canada and Australia. As the world of Moorcroft expanded, a new ethos crept into its way of life. Customers would not come to the Works and hurl themselves through the door. Instead, Moorcroft Pottery went out to find its customers and invite them in. At the same time it pushed the quality of its work further and further up-market, to a level where it actually entered the devastating recession of the early 1990's in good commercial shape.

Today, Hugh will remark happily that Moorcroft enjoyed its recession. Throughout those dreadful years, it showed growth in excess of twenty per cent per annum. While others were shedding labour, Moorcroft was recruiting. During Moorcroft's dark days of 1986, staff levels had fallen to sixteen. Only two years later the total exceeded forty, and by 1996 staff levels had risen yet again to eighty-seven. It was, however, in 1988 that Moorcroft received its own financial accolade, featuring in the centre pages of 'Bankground', the in-house magazine of National Westminster Bank Plc, as a model recovery worth talking about in commercial and banking terms. National Westminster Bank had been Moorcroft's bankers for

FACING: Inset: Pattie Booth, a 94 year-old former decorator, talks to her successors two generations later in the Moorcroft decorating shop before refurbishment. Main picture: Wendy Mason (centre) painting a 5″ Phoenix vase in the decorating shop after refurbishment.

seventy-three years, but Edwards hardly looked at the article. In it, Richard and he remained in the background. The bankers held the pots. A few weeks later the arrival of a Channel Four News team sent to investigate the Moorcroft recovery caused much more of a stir at the Works, and for the first time Moorcroft staff discovered what adjustments were required to accommodate a television crew.

With the success and the publicity came tensions, and with the tensions there followed stress. In May 1992, the Edwards and Dennises decided to run the Tokyo Trade Fair themselves. For Hugh and Maureen it was to be a mix of work and holiday, and the fulfilment of a lifetime's dream to visit the ancient Japanese capital of Kyoto. It was a good trip, with a few days rest in Hong Kong for the four of them as the guests of Hugh's Partners in Richards Butler's Hong Kong office en route. After the close of the successful Tokyo Trade Show, the two couples planned to travel independently. They went their separate ways, the Edwards to Kyoto and the Dennises on an ambitious tour of northern Japan.

The Edwards returned to the United Kingdom first. A week later a card arrived from the Dennises featuring a pure white pot without a trace of design. The message on the reverse was ambiguous. 'Moorcroft Pottery 1993? Love Richard and Sally'. Hugh took the card to be a joke. Maureen feared that it was serious, suggesting that the white pot might herald the beginning of the end of the Dennises' involvement in Moorcroft. A possible interpretation was that no design meant no designers.

THREE

Christmas Revelations

On Saturday, 5 December 1992, Richard Dennis telephoned Hugh Edwards to tell him that both he and his wife, Sally, had decided to leave Moorcroft and sell their shares. Between 5 and 23 December, Hugh tried to persuade the Dennises to change their minds. However, on 23 December, immediately after the Moorcroft Annual General Meeting, Richard and Sally formally announced their departure. Before six months had passed, the lawyers had earned their fees and the Moorcroft design team had gone!

Christmas 1992 had suddenly become a time of change, and the consequences of the departure of the design team mixed incongruously with the festive season. Fortunately, the 1993 sales catalogue had been printed and dispatched to Moorcroft retailers. The catalogue apart, however, the design team had also undertaken all Moorcroft publishing and printing as part of their responsibilities. Since he had joined the company, Richard Dennis had regarded Moorcroft printing and publishing as his preserve, and with justification. A series of successful books on English ceramics which Richard had published bore ample testimony to that. In amongst the bustle and confusion of Christmas there had exploded, like a bolt from the blue, the problem of the search for a replacement designer, not to mention a reorganisation of the quality printing and publishing so essential in the presentation of the Moorcroft image to the world of retailers and their customers, collectors and auction houses alike.

Moorcroft had known only three full-time designers in ninety-five years. As with printing and publishing, Hugh and Maureen Edwards and John and Gill Moorcroft had generally steered well clear of involvement in the creative processes of design. Throughout history, all designers it seemed guarded their preserves closely, and intruders were soon chased away. Indeed, Hugh Edwards often recalled the story of one eminent Dutch pottery operating during the last century where the chief designer, himself one of the proprietors of the business, had been savage and ruthless with anything which remotely smacked of competition. Those concerned never stayed around long, whether as a decorator aspiring to more glorious horizons or, in another case, when an accounts clerk had the effrontery to suggest one or two items on a particular design were capable of modest improvement. Perhaps the Dutch were different a hundred years ago. It was an interesting line of thought and one which crossed Hugh Edwards' mind more than once over Christmas. More importantly, he was impatient to start the search for a new designer.

Sally and Richard had clearly done all they could to prepare Moorcroft for the 1993 season. The catalogue had been printed, but the first item on the missing list was the large prestige vase, hitherto produced in a limited edition and crucial for Moorcroft's profile at the International Spring Fairs at Birmingham and Frankfurt. Also missing was the third in a series of five planned ginger jars made specially for B. & W. Thornton, Moorcroft retailers in Stratford-upon-Avon. Previous pieces made for Thornton's had, not surprisingly, been based on Shakespearian themes, and Edwards quickly resigned himself to a renewed study of Shakespeare as essential Christmas reading.

Once the design started to move towards production things started to go wrong. Further kiln trials involving the use of red tube-lining on the design team's prototype Fuchsia vase for the Moorcroft Collectors' Club had begun to manifest symptoms suggesting future production difficulties. More worrying still were early signs of more widespread technical problems in the chemical structure of the 1993 Special Occasions White Rose vase. Both designs were pretty, but neither was ready for production. Both pieces required further trials, and there was a distinct possibility that both might have to go back to the drawing board. On that Edwards was clear. What had seemed at first blush like a complete design presentation for 1993 might just have fallen rather short after production trials had been completed. Time was short, too.

Maureen Edwards had taken the Dennises' decision to leave Moorcroft rather less dramatically than her husband. Although upset at their departure, she accepted that their decision marked the end of an era, and that it was time for Moorcroft to move on. Her reasoning was based on more than logic. More than eighteen months earlier she, not Hugh, had sat through a curious interview at the Works. At that time orders were fast outstripping the capacity of Moorcroft to meet them. Richard Dennis had suggested it might be in the company's best interest to advertise in a different way for the five new decorators the company needed to recruit. Instead of the ordinary and unimaginative advertisements which Moorcroft traditionally produced on such occasions, calling simply for

FACING: *Moorcroft shapes reintroduced 1987–92*

'decorators' or 'tube-liners', the new wording asked for decorators and tube-liners who could 'both paint and draw'.

The new advertisement requested successful candidates for interview to bring along portfolios of drawings and samples of their ceramic art work. The response had been instantaneous and enormous. Instead of the usual half dozen bored responses Edwards expected, more than one hundred and forty applicants, ranging from experienced ceramics decorators to graduates in almost every field of the applied arts, sent in their curricula vitae. Indeed, it would have been hard to find an artistic qualification whose possessor had not responded to the advertisement. Three days were needed to read and whittle down applications to a modest twenty selected for interview. The interviews themselves took place over two days, with ten candidates seen on each day.

It had been a matter of considerable irritation to Hugh that he could interview on only one of the two days, but Maureen had stayed on, and together with the Dennises and Moorcrofts had completed the task. Five candidates were eventually employed. It was a matter of concern to those involved in the interviews that so much fine artistic talent lay on the scrap heap of redundancy brought about by the recession. As a result, every applicant interviewed received a personal letter from John Moorcroft regretting or congratulating as the occasion required. John has a good turn of phrase, and throughout his life an unfailing ability to be courteous and kind has never deserted him.

There had been one candidate who Edwards had felt merited a personal letter. Not that he had interviewed Rachel Bishop nor indeed had even seen examples of her work, but his wife, who is seldom deceived by anything and has a rare and instinctive insight into a person's capability or lack of it, had been impressed. Just as significant, in the portfolio of Rachel's work John Moorcroft had seen distant echoes of the design qualities of his father, William. For her part, Maureen Edwards had felt that instinctive collector's shiver which told her that Rachel Bishop understood the very essence of Moorcroft pottery.

Maureen always reacted as a collector, and generous words of approval of Rachel's work spoken by Richard Dennis during the interview confirmed that the antiques dealer had also been moved. Gill Moorcroft, an avid collector herself, had also been impressed but said little. Rachel's wild flowers had simplicity and beauty; her butterflies carried in their delicate wings a strength of line mixed with colour and grace. But cold reality had brought the appreciation party to an abrupt halt. A designer was not what the Board was looking for. Moorcroft had no need for a new designer. In Sally, the company already had a very competent designer of its own, and Rachel Bishop was rejected without further discussion.

In writing his personal letter to Rachel, Edwards had listened to the reports of those present about her interview. Since he had not seen Rachel himself, it was crucial that he gather as much information about her as he could. The letter ultimately was relatively short: some members of the Board had been impressed with her work, and as a result he would like to keep in touch with her career progress. On and off during the ensuing months, Rachel Bishop and Hugh Edwards had corresponded, with the letters all neatly filed away by Edwards' secretary, Jo Rogers. In his filing cabinets there were dozens of Moorcroft files, but Edwards knew that Jo would know exactly which file contained the Bishop correspondence.

As if reading her husband's thoughts, Maureen had suggested that Rachel Bishop might be as good a starting point as any other in the search for a designer. The Moorcrofts in exchanging Christmas greetings on the telephone the following day, had confirmed Maureen's thinking. Gill, as always, wondered why an approach had not already been made. To track down a person called Bishop in Hampshire over Christmas proved more than a simple task, but even so, on the day after Boxing Day, Rachel Bishop was sitting in the Edwards' lounge.

Interview portfolio: study of butterfly by Rachel Bishop

FOUR

Call for a Bishop

John Moorcroft was troubled. The cause of John's unease was pansies. It was not that he particularly liked pansies as a flower, but in the middle of 1992 the design team had agreed to produce a range of pansies for the 1993 season. With this decision under his belt, John had travelled round the southern island of New Zealand, a large slice of Australia and significant parts of the United States and Canada announcing, rather like a Moorcroft John the Baptist, the re-arrival of pansies.

From the early years of the century through to the late 1930's, pansies had been used in William Moorcroft's designs with only a few variations of tone and ground colour. Their large, broad-faced petals gave great scope for a decorator who was something more than a colour technician, and some very fine pieces were made over the period as a result. In 1972, Walter was tempted to design a pansy range as a result of subtle pressure from the American market. However, Pansy Nouveau failed to capture the imagination of collectors, and dogged by technical problems the range was discontinued only a year later.

The Board's decision at the end of June to re-introduce Pansies for a third time had been a sensible one. Sally's recent designs in general, and Cluny in particular, had leaned heavily on tube-lining for effect. The results of this had been considerable and strongly-vocalised stress among the Moorcroft tube-liners, with an occasional surplus painting capacity among the Moorcroft decorators, five or six of whom were periodically without work to do as a result. At a time when the company had more orders than it could cope with, the sight of idle decorators in the decorating shop had been bizarre. The simple Moorcroft proposition had always been that the more detailed the tube-lining, the easier became the decorator's task. The Moorcroft Board had decided to produce a 'painting' range of pottery, as opposed to a 'tube-lining' range of pottery, to adjust that imbalance, with pansies the chosen flower. By their own high standards, the first trials of the design

FACING: *Rachel Bishop at work, 1996*

team's pansy pots had not been a success. Other pressures had apparently slowed down the design team's Pansy project to such an extent that the 1993 catalogue had gone to press without featuring a single new range for the first time since the Dennises' arrival in 1986.

New tube-liners had been included in the latest recruitment drive in order to feed more work to the decorators and release the pressures on the existing tube-liners. It takes a year to train a single Moorcroft tube-liner, and if the problem was to be solved by recruiting more staff it would be a considerable time before the imbalance between tube-lining and painting had been corrected. John Moorcroft knew this in just the same way he understood that the pansy was a difficult flower from which to create a design. It would take a great effort by a designer of consummate quality to create a good pansy design, and the vast increase in the colour spectrum of pansies available since the First World War had made the job even more difficult. William Moorcroft had had only three basic pansy colours to chose from: blue/purple, cream and maroon. John knew this and explained patiently to all Moorcroft customers who enquired not only why the new pansy range had failed to materialize, but also why a design using pansies today was more difficult to create than it had been even twenty years earlier.

Gill Moorcroft was sympathetic, but found herself with a different but no less serious problem of her own. Sally's pretty Fuchsia vase, designed for the Collectors' Club for 1993, involved a novel use of red tube-lining which was causing serious technical problems. For almost a hundred years tube-lining had been the traditional Moorcroft method of applying design through the medium of liquid clay to the raw clay of an unfired pot, a process not unlike putting decorative icing on a cake.

By adding red oxide dye to the slip in accordance with the design, the viscous quality of the liquid clay had been impaired. As a result, it flowed from the tube-liner's pipettes onto the trial pots for a maximum of two centimetres before 'breaking'. After firing this meant the tube-lining became intermittent under the glaze, and the breaks were singularly unappealing. Additionally, in firing the red dye tended to 'bleed' onto the body of the vase. In the sometimes perverse way of art pottery, this 'fault' was not unattractive. Gill had gone out of her way to be exceptionally patient with the Moorcroft Works Manager, Justin Emery, over the technical difficulties he faced. After taking advice from almost every available source in Stoke-on-Trent, even Justin the colour expert eventually had to concede

FACING: *Drawings from Rachel Bishop's interview portfolio*

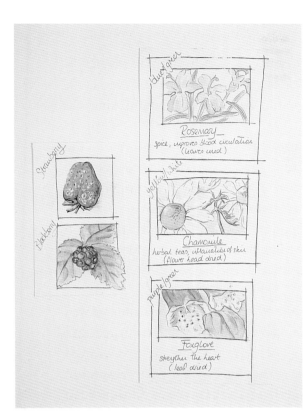

Strawberry

Blackberry

Rosemary
spice, improves blood circulation
(leaves used)

Chamomile
herbal teas, inflamations of skin
(flower head dried)

Foxglove
strenghten the heart
(leaf dried)

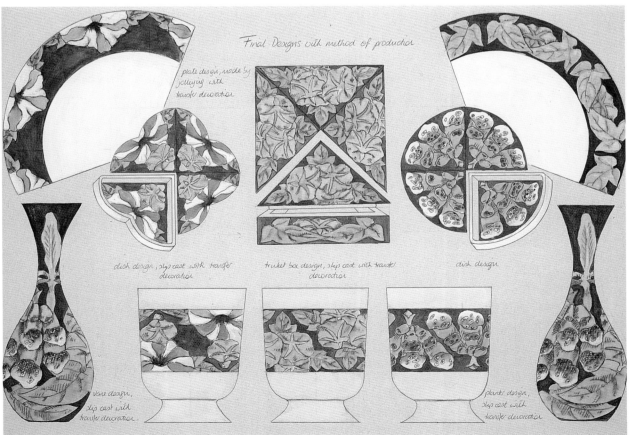

Final Designs with method of production

plate design, made by
jolleying with
transfer decoration

dish design, slip cast with transfer
decoration

trinket box design, slip cast with transfer
decoration

dish design

vase design,
slip cast with
transfer decoration.

plant design,
slip cast with
transfer decoration.

defeat. The Fuchsia vase with the red tube-lining was unsuitable for production. As a result, without a designer to call on, Gill too had a serious problem.

There were a few things which Hugh and Maureen ought to know, Gill told John. Most important was that neither she nor her husband saw any reason for resorting to nepotism to select a Moorcroft designer. Gill was adamant that the Edwards should know that. Nepotism was not, and never had been, part of her personal philosophy. If there existed anywhere a designer called 'Moorcroft', the name alone was not enough. The new designer had to be the very best that could be found: a person who was comfortable working to a standard of excellence in the Moorcroft idiom – whatever their name might happen to be. As was her habit, she came straight to the point, suggesting that Hugh telephone the promising young designer from Hampshire.

Gill had to concede that since Hugh had not even met Rachel Bishop, it was important that he did so as soon as possible. The consensus between the Edwards and the Moorcrofts was that if Rachel Bishop wanted to become the new designer at Moorcroft, and only the fourth in almost one hundred years at that, she would have to take the opportunity and re-organise her life around the proposition. To this day, Hugh Edwards still has residual bouts of conscience in relation to Rachel's employers at the time he made his telephone call.

Caution had always been one of the hallmarks of Moorcroft family character, and John Moorcroft was no exception to this general rule. He took great pains to suggest that the new designer's contract should be non-exclusive; that initially at least, the new designer should work on a commission basis and be paid a fixed fee for each completed task. Only when Rachel (if it was to be Rachel at all) had proved herself worthy of the Moorcroft design mantle by designing a marketable range of pottery, should the responsibility of its weight be placed upon her shoulders. Since such thoughts tied in well with the Edwards' view of the future, John was happy. Hugh was ready to see Rachel for the first time himself. Although he was not to know it at the time, what amounted to an extended interview lasting many months was about to start.

Hugh Edwards had interviewed many people in his life, and for him first impressions were the most important. Rachel's handshake was firm and her eyes looked directly at the person with whom she was speaking. So far so good! Strength and direction were present, both useful weapons to have in your armoury when confronted by an occasionally uncooperative Works Manager. As a breed, Works Managers tend to dislike designers. Designers flounce and flap, provoke drama and destroy order, discipline and routine. At the other end of the scale, the fact that Rachel was twenty-four years old, only two weeks older than the Edwards' son, Richard, was neither here nor there. Moorcroft Pottery was already in the mood to prepare itself for the next generation, and design was a good place to start.

In his public life as a commercial lawyer, Hugh played a role which he enjoyed less and less as the years ground their dull and dreary way past him. In his private life he was a ceramics connoisseur and, more especially, a single-minded collector of Moorcroft pottery. At a personal level he identified himself with every Moorcroft collector; he enjoyed their company, understood what motivated them and, above all, was prepared to take their criticisms. To that extent, Moorcroft collectors constitute a very important, select body of people, united by their ability to accept or reject a pot by the feel of its lines at their finger tips and the stir it creates inside them on seeing it for the first time. Not that he would admit it, but Edwards had held his breath at the moment Rachel Bishop opened the portfolio of her work for him to look at.

Whether it was the butterflies or the wild flowers which had so moved his colleagues earlier, the tile designs that leaned heavily towards William Morris without actually touching him, the harebells, the lilies or the foxgloves, it mattered not. Every page carried the pure essence of Moorcroft: strength of line and colour, each using or reflecting natural form in all its aspects. And that was only part of it! Rachel Bishop was a ceramicist, schooled in clay, its variable shades and textures. Like Walter Moorcroft and his father William before him, Rachel drew directly onto the curved surface of the unfired pots. Her degree and postgraduate experience were formal recognition of the contents of every page of the Rachel Bishop portfolio.

Now Edwards understood what had so moved those interviewing Rachel more than eighteen months previously. This young designer was special. At the end of what had started as a dull December day, Rachel selected and took away with her to use as a model a large white vase from the Edwards' home dating back to the early 1920's. Her commission was to design to its shape the prestige piece to be introduced at the Birmingham International Spring Fair scheduled to open in less than six weeks time.

John and Gill had stayed within a few feet of their telephone all afternoon, and it was John who pounced when the call came through. Yes, Rachel appeared to have great quality; yes, she had been given the prestige vase commission as agreed;

yes, she was still in employment elsewhere and unlikely to leave it until a full-time job was offered; yes, Edwards appreciated that it was a recession and only a very brave and ambitious person would give up a secure job in return for a commission, with only the vaguest promise of more to come.

Reflection would probably force John to admit that the next few days were among the busiest of his life. Within an hour of Edwards' call he had organised the Works Salesman to collect the battered and cracked white vase from Hampshire, as soon as Rachel had finished recording its contours. Ten minutes later he telephoned Moorcroft mould-maker, Trevor Critchlow, placing him on urgent standby to profile, model, block and case the new vase before the Moorcroft Works re-opened after the Christmas break. Finally, he called up Works Manager, Justin Emery, and without pausing either for breath or thought exacted a promise of staggering proportions to give total priority to what was to become the famous Moorcroft Tigris vase.

FIVE

New Team

It had been a matter of some sadness for Edwards to decline the invitation to field his President's Eleven on New Year's Day 1993 against the Saffron Walden Hockey Club's First Eleven. The race against time at Moorcroft had become more important, and in any event the Saffron Walden President had lost his very able goalkeeper to the same cause. John Moorcroft had another side to his personality, one which tied him to Hugh in terms of friendship in a totally different way. Both of them had been more than competent hockey players in their younger days, and both were still enthusiastic veterans and prominent members of their respective local clubs. As a result, it was not altogether surprising that Hugh had been in the habit of calling on the veteran goalkeeper from the North Stafford Hockey Club to turn out once a year on New Year's Day to play for his President's Eleven.

The previous year the pitch had been muddy. A violent assault on the President's goal by a teaming hoard of enthusiastic young men had caused John to bring off an amazing save – amazing not only because he stopped a stinging shot, but also because after being knocked to the ground John had sat on the ball which promptly vanished into the mud. Why that rather funny, unrelated event prompted the word 'centenary' to flash into Edwards' mind, he was to never know. The thought had been tenacious, however, and had recurred periodically throughout the remainder of 1992.

His potential non-appearance at the 1993 President's match had caused Edwards to brood over Christmas and the New Year on the prospect of the Moorcroft centenary even more seriously than before. Not only was the need for another top quality designer urgent: that designer had to have the calibre and strength of purpose to respond to the demands that a centenary year would undoubtedly entail. The design work would be undertaken during the two preceding years, and perhaps even earlier if museums and auction houses were to be involved. No other art pottery had survived for a hundred years and still remained in independent family ownership. The Martin Brothers had produced their individual wares for 42 years, William De Morgan for 36 years, Ruskin for 35 years, Pilkington Royal Lancastrian for 47 years in its original form, Bernard Moore for 10 years, whereas Doulton and Wedgwood would certainly not wish to be called art potteries today. Moorcroft was unique; a surviving dinosaur of the art world which ought to have become extinct long since.

Edwards was glad that John had invited him to join the company almost seven years earlier, yet sad that his own invitees, Richard and Sally Dennis, had left. Inevitably the two of them would miss the pleasure of direct involvement in the centenary celebrations, and Edwards was unhappy about that. Indeed, centenary thoughts had been on his mind as he talked to Rachel Bishop during that grey, misty day after Christmas in 1992. She had spoken knowledgably about William Morris, enquiring intelligently about the similarities between William De Morgan's style and the Windsor Carnation vase produced by Moorcroft in an edition of 300 for one of its enthusiastic young retailers, Talents of Windsor, led by Yvonne Hayward and Ian Herrod. Rachel's reaction to the photographs of the underside of the arch to the main gate of the Emperor's palace in Kyoto, the ancient capital of Japan, had been interesting. The young designer had recognised the De Morgan images in the Kyoto gate, and Edwards half-hoped she would offer to work the Kyoto images onto a pot or two; but the conversation passed on to other things.

Back in 1986 when they had joined the company, the Dennises had moved forward from a cold start. In those days Hugh and Richard believed that the market was hungry for change. With the youngest Moorcroft design at least ten years old and the oldest design more than sixty years old, collectors would have become bored. By 1992, however, renewed interest in Moorcroft had become as sophisticated as it was strong. Sally had set high standards, and for the new designer there would never be the luxury of turning back the clock. To succeed, the new designer would have to take Moorcroft's art on the run, and Moorcroft's best-selling Cluny range would be the starting point, not the goal.

It was Gill Moorcroft who dubbed Rachel's first large vase the Tigris vase. A clever name, Hugh thought at the time: a cross between Tiger Lily and Iris. He had been much less sure about the vase itself. It was different, yet familiar, and it failed to stir his Moorcroft instincts as much as he would have liked. For John, it was simply a vase; it arrived on time and was something to talk about during the Spring Fair at Birmingham and later at Frankfurt. More significantly, John had put in a

FACING: *Tigris vase: Height 16"*

great deal of personal effort to ensure that the first two prototypes had passed through all stages of manufacture in sufficient time to be wrapped in bubblewrap and delivered to the National Exhibition Centre on the back seat of his car.

Walter Moorcroft, John's elder brother, had seen the first prototype of the Tigris vase as soon as the firing truck came out of the kiln, and had judged the design style as being close to his own. Directly from her interview portfolio, Rachel had taken a combination of different kinds of lily and a strongly drawn iris. Walter Moorcroft had himself used lilies with great effect in some of his earlier designs. Maybe that was the answer. Hugh was not quite sure. Rachel had perhaps assumed, wrongly, that the departure of the Dennis design team had been welcome, and she had perhaps also assumed, again wrongly, that what was being sought was a return to traditional Moorcroft design features of the post-war years, of which Walter was both author and custodian. What Hugh had failed to grasp was an alternative option, namely that the Tigris design reflected youth and that most personal of all design qualities – Rachel's own style, which he had seen so clearly and unambiguously presented in her interview portfolio.

On the strength of the quality of the Tigris vase, there had been a consensus between the Moorcrofts and the Edwards that Rachel should proceed with a second independent commission. B. & W. Thornton of Stratford-upon-Avon had become Moorcroft retailers, operating from two shops, one close to Shakespeare's birth place and the other only a short walk from the Swan Theatre. Nobody had any real idea of how Sally Tuffin had worked up her ideas for the Thornton projects, and Hugh concluded that a personal visit was called for. All Sally's design work at Moorcroft had been done under her maiden name Tuffin, and Hugh decided it would have been Sally Tuffin rather than Sally Dennis who would have visited Thornton's shop. For her part Rachel had organised leave of absence from her current employers to attend the Birmingham International Spring Fair, which opened on the first Sunday in February 1993 at the National Exhibition Centre. As a result, everyone agreed that Hugh should travel to Stratford-upon-Avon from Birmingham with Rachel and Alan Wright.

After the usual social pleasantries, Edwards had been startled when Barry Thornton (the 'B' in B. & W. Thornton) produced a pencil sketch of a possible design taken from a theme in Shakespeare's play, 'The Winter's Tale'. Guy Thornton, who was responsible for the sketch, was a very competent artist, and Barry was clearly pleased with his son's work. Edwards had no clue as to whether or not this had been a repeat performance of an act played out before the Moorcroft de-

sign team the previous year or whether the Thornton family had come to the conclusion that as Moorcroft had no designer it perhaps needed a helping hand!
Either way, it was an awkward situation for Rachel. Here was a retail customer
offering a specific idea for discussion driven by Guy Thornton's comprehensive
knowledge of Shakespeare and ability to draw.

Rachel had had no involvement whatsoever in dealing with Moorcroft's customers, and Edwards took the initiative. Some modification of the design would
be necessary if it was to be successfully translated into the Moorcroft idiom.
Although cleverly drawn, Hugh suggested, the crescent moon might look like a
flying banana, whilst the round image of the sun might mutate into a flying orange
on a pot. Moorcroft had already had experience of both! Barry Thornton agreed,
and out came the sun and the crescent moon. The straight lines featured in Guy's
sketch would be difficult for the tube-liners, and as a result there would be inevitable technical disappointment. At this point Rachel, recovering from her earlier
shock at the production of the sketch, took up some of the running and suggested
the substitution of iris leaves for the straight lines. Guy Thornton agreed.

Edwards had already learned just how difficult it was to design an image and
then convert that image into Moorcroft's unique ceramic art in the same way that
he recognised in Guy's work the sensitive reaction of a good artist to the powerful
images provoked by Shakespeare's prose. Colour, of course, was an open question
since Guy's was only a pencil sketch. Both Guy and his father were happy with
Rachel's comment that the drawing provoked interesting
ideas in terms of colour. Rachel was given a free hand as to
that. Later, Edwards had to admit that he had made a significant mistake. When Rachel took up the colour challenge, she did so in a way that made the most complex of
her predecessor's efforts look positively modest. Moorcroft colours are derived from metallic oxides, cobalt
(blue), iron (red), and so on. Sometimes the base metals
are incompatible, and in the white hot heat of the kiln metallic incompatibility can cause a colour to disappear altogether with disastrous consequences for the pot and its design. An understanding of metallic oxides is as much part
of the Moorcroft technique as the working of colour and an
ability to draw. Rachel's inexperience in the use of Moorcroft's oxide colours at that time resulted in a Ginger Jar

'The Winter's Tale' ginger jar,
1993: Height 6"

which required thirteen colour 'builds'. The previous record had been nine, and it is said that the howls of the Works Manager can still be heard echoing in the rafters at the Works today. No piece of pottery in the pages of Moorcroft history has ever been produced at such a catastrophic financial loss.

It was raining hard by the time Edwards returned to the car park with Rachel and Alan. Generally speaking, Alan Wright had been reasonably pleased with the way the discussion had gone. He was an experienced tactician who knew exactly what to say at precisely the right time. Edwards was less sanguine, and his feeling of uncertainty later increased when Gill Moorcroft suggested that Rachel be commissioned to redesign the Collectors' Club vase.

Everything was coming in a rush, and Edwards' uncertainty matured into serious unease. Rachel might turn out to be one huge mistake, and that would be bad for Moorcroft. At least on the sales front all was going well. The Spring Fair at Birmingham closed with a flourish, and the new collection of small vases on new shapes across the ranges had provoked a lively interest among Moorcroft's retail customers. Edwards had pushed hard to introduce new shapes after the Roger Michell initiative, and the collection of small vases was an innovation pursued with that intense determination for which he had already become well-known and which irritated some, intimidated others and pleased the remainder.

An extension to the Works had become another urgent priority. The decorating strength at Moorcroft would have to be further increased to cope with the volume of orders which the Birmingham Spring Fair suggested would be the pattern for the months ahead. The Tigris vase, while not walking away into orders, had sold very well indeed. The small vase collection had been introduced for collectors, and happily for Edwards each piece was in demand. Richard Dennis, the ceramics dealer, had supported him on the introduction of the small vases and on many other issues in the past, but he would no longer be in Birmingham as a Moorcroft shareholder. Deep inside Edwards' mind there had been the hope, quietly nurtured, that the Tigris vase would sell at record levels, but hope alone does not sell a piece of art pottery. It is necessary to spread the gospel about its attributes and its story.

Salesmen Alan Wright and Steven Swann were stirred into action. Harold Bowen, Moorcroft's photographer in Stoke-on-Trent, took an exceptionally fine shot of the Tigris vase, and it was given a high profile in the May edition of the Collectors' Club Newsletter. Collectors themselves were quietly mobilised; magazines and newspapers were fed with copy. Like a bush fire the word was suddenly about: someone new was designing for Moorcroft, and by the middle of 1993 the Tigris vase, in a limited edition of 150, had sold out. All those concerned had every reason to be pleased with the result. In what at first blush might have appeared a casual afterthought, Edwards urged the sales team to continue their momentum and sell out the remaining pieces of the former design team's large 1992 Rainforest limited edition vase. Not even fired clay, however beautiful, will move unless you can convince collectors of its quality. The iron will of John's father and his consummate ability to keep the general public aware of his work had carried Moorcroft through two world wars. In comparison, the change of designer showed every sign of becoming little more than a modest skirmish. However, the design team had been more than designers.

As well as being an antiques dealer, over many years Richard Dennis had been responsible for publishing a number of first-class books on English ceramics. He knew how to choose and use his authors, how to find printers and typesetters well-schooled in his way of thinking, and graphic designers and photographers who understood his directions. If they all lived in Somerset, so much the better. During their years at Moorcroft the Dennises had taken responsibility for much of the company's printing and publishing.

Edwards had first experienced the Dennis publishing techniques during their successful partnership in producing two editions as well as a revision of Paul Atterbury's book, *Moorcroft*. The memory of the Edwards' family home transforming itself into a photographic studio was still fresh in his mind: the airing cupboard used as a dark room; a huge quantity of valuable old pots travelling from all over London and many other parts of the British Isles; the continual fear of damage and the elation at each high-quality transparency. The proof-reading of a text printed in Japan some months later had been a different kind of unforgettable experience. Over two hundred errors in spelling, sentence construction and punctuation required correction.

But after the first edition, all of the 'hands-on' excitement had disappeared. Edwards had felt that his role had been systematically reduced to that of a simple provider of cheques, half of which Richard had promptly repaid as soon as sales receipts from the book had permitted. Both Hugh and Maureen had felt hurt by this apparent shift in responsibilities. What Richard had failed to notice was that his partner had no real stomach for finance and commerce. If a person does something well, it does not necessarily follow that they enjoy doing it. Commercial expertise had been willingly offered, and the bank had always been persuaded to advance the cash required for publication. That was Edwards' contribution, but he derived little pleasure from providing it. He carried in his mind the lingering thought that he had been manoeuvred further and further away from the pure fascination derived from the process of publication. With two editions of 5,000 copies each, the successful sell-out of both within five years was reassuring. Edwards had no commercial anxieties about the first reprint of the second edition, but the fun of close involvement had gone. As a result, he had been exceptionally pleased when John and Gill had turned to Maureen and suggested she assume the role of in-house publisher at Moorcroft.

Preparation of photographs for the 1994 sales catalogue would remain with John. Everybody was agreed about that. John's unfussy approach, based on the simple need for the pots to sell themselves, without dressing, had been a feature of Moorcroft catalogues for a number of years. John had never liked the idea of swags of pearls hanging limply around the neck of a pot or the pots themselves languishing carelessly on a draped silk or velvet ground. Overdressing, in John's book of rules, had always been synonymous with bad taste or eccentricity.

Needing no encouragement, Maureen Edwards first took control of the Collectors' Club Newsletter. Until that moment she had always felt herself to be the spare pair of hands at Moorcroft. Now those hands were needed in a very central way, and she set to work. Fraser Street was approached and readily agreed to write a further article. Hugh volunteered an appreciation of Richard and Sally. One of Maureen's more disreputable contacts offered an 'antiques' angle to collecting under the name 'Millie Millward'. Searching through some of her late mother-in-law Hazel's personal papers, Gill Moorcroft had discovered a moving letter written in the late 1920's from William Moorcroft to his fiancée and future second wife. John Shorter in Australia volunteered to write an historical piece. The auction houses and the dealers all pulled together, and with an original contribution from the 78 year old Walter Moorcroft, the May issue of the 1993 Collectors' Club Newsletter was ready for publication.

Moving in parallel, Maureen had also written and printed a flyer for the new Thornton ginger jar, The Winter's Tale – still proving a nightmare in production terms. The new Moorcroft publisher tracked down a quality printer in Bishops Stortford whose quotation had a good competitive edge. Richard Dennis had always been keen on prices, and it was felt to be something of a triumph, Maureen admitted later, to produce a Newsletter with more content and at a lower cost than its predecessors. As a precaution, Edwards had warned the Board that his wife was always late. He need not have worried. Only three days later than the same issue for the previous year, copies were mailed to collectors all over the world. Within days the collectors' own responses began to arrive at the Works, and the consensus was that the May 1993 Newsletter was without doubt the best yet.

Never one to adopt a posture of praise for long, Gill was forced to reconsider her own outstanding problem. For some weeks she had been worrying almost continuously about the still-non-existent 1993 Collectors' Club vase. During a follow-up visit to Thornton's at Stratford-upon-Avon, Rachel had shown Hugh Edwards the first of her trials for an alternative Collectors' Club vase. The presentation to Guy and Barry Thornton had been less than satisfactory, or at least that was Edwards' opinion. For the second time, too, it had rained, and the walk back to the car park had been even wetter than on the previous occasion. Rachel's first trials for the 1993 Collectors' Club vase could not have been presented in a worse light, coming as they did out of the boot of a car on that dismal Saturday afternoon.

1993 Collectors' Club Fuchsia vase: Height 6″

Rachel had used the 80/6″ shape just as her predecessor had done, and had drawn on it a flower which Edwards cruelly suggested looked like a shrivelled clematis with a starfish emblem at the centre. The vases were, in Edwards' view, rubbish – and he said so. The following year Rachel admitted to Hugh that she had taken the trials home and had placed them on the cistern in the toilet at her house to reflect one of the more choice words he had used. It had not been the right time or place to talk about Collectors' Club vases, but Rachel had the strength of purpose to persevere with this strong-willed lawyer. His eyes spelt out what he hoped would be a new challenge when he suggested that Rachel should stay with a Fuchsia design and consign traditional Moorcroft, represented by anything that resembled clematis, with or without a starfish in the centre, to its proper place in history. Much later Rachel pointed out that the hapless flower was supposed to be morning glory and not clematis at all!

In June 1993 at Moorcroft's Open Weekend auction, Peter Blood, the auctioneer and a well-known personality in the Potteries, had been startled when Sally Dennis' red tube-lined trial Fuchsia vase, all six inches of it, had been hammered down for £210. His surprise turned to astonishment when Rachel Bishop's first Fuchsia trial for the 1993 Collectors' Club vase on the same shape sold for £480. Edwards was happy, the competitor in him genuinely pleased at the warm and spontaneous outburst of applause from collectors when the hammer fell for Rachel's piece. When on the following day Rachel's second trial piece sold for £520, and all her other trial vases in the 6″ to 8″ range sold for prices between £180 and £350, Edwards' competitive instincts were satisfied. Moorcroft collectors had

Maureen Edwards checks the proof of the Fuchsia vase

taken the new young designer to their hearts, and they were the most reliable judges of her artistic ability.

Dark clouds had earlier threatened the arrival of the Rachel Bishop Fuchsia vase. In the early stages of experimentation Works Manager, Justin Emery, had been almost worryingly co-operative. Gill had put his compliant demeanour down to the fact that as the vase had only four colour 'builds', it was a production model to be encouraged. Sadly, Harold Bowen's photograph of the Fuchsia vase had not been one of his better efforts, and Maureen was given a bad time at the printers as a result. She had been keen that her first 'flyer' to be mailed to Moorcroft collectors worldwide would be of good quality. The background colour of the first batch, as

Gill was quick to point out, had been printed with colour tones ranging from fawn to olive green. Under most circumstances, this would have entitled Moorcroft to reject the batch. However, since neither Hugh nor Maureen had been able to spell the word 'Fuchsia', the printers had happily reproduced the incorrect spelling four thousand times in a variable colourway. They were equally happy to rerun the same quantity with the correct spelling.

So far the prospective printing cost had done no more than double, but when the variable colourway reappeared for a second time, the printers were confronted with the fearsome sight of Maureen Edwards, solicitor, both brown eyes well and truly blazing. The third print run turned out to be a sombre affair. A sample Fuchsia vase sat precariously on the printing machine with an apprehensive printing works proprietor and a very angry lawyer supervising the process. Not even Gill Moorcroft could find fault with the third batch, and ten weeks after mailing the Fuchsia flyer, twice the number of Moorcroft Collectors had ordered vases than had done so on any previous occasion.

Yvonne Haywood of Talents of Windsor presenting a
Moorcroft vase to H.M. The Queen in June 1996

SIX

Oberon

In April 1991, Hugh Edwards had been elected to the Board of the international law firm, Richards Butler. Election to the Board of a firm of solicitors with more than six hundred employees in five different countries necessarily involved spending a considerable amount of time on administrative matters. His work at Moorcroft since September 1986 was acknowledged to have radically changed his relationship with his own commercial clients. For the first time in his career, Edwards had been forced to practice what he preached. He had found out how people in business made mistakes. He learned that success was built on a mix of experience, vision and the will to make things happen. Most significantly of all, in his professional life Edwards now knew what it was like to be a client.

After his involvement with Moorcroft his professional attitude to his clients began to reflect his own experiences. He understood a client's anxieties and how to help them achieve their objectives. It was this capacity which his partners at Richards Butler recognised as an asset to the firm. From the outset, his commitment to Moorcroft had been the subject of formal approval from his partners, but once that approval had been given, as long as he earned his fees, looked after his clients and made his required contribution, his partners had been happy and supportive.

What Edwards had not taken into consideration was the sudden retirement of the head of his department. In a large law firm like Richards Butler, not only did its various offices worldwide run as quasi-independent businesses, but in the firm's City office there were four large sub-groups or departments, each having its own specialisation. For a firm with a good worldwide reputation and clients varying from national governments to airlines, ships to factories and cinemas to banks, it had been Edwards' good fortune to belong to the Property Group. Under the leadership of John Rainford, a solicitor of remarkable academic and practical

FACING: *The Rainford charger: Diameter 14". Presented 1993.*

achievement, the Property Group had moved from strength to strength over the two previous decades. Their research into bank lending trends and the impact of the recession years of 1990-93 on commercial leasing had been acknowledged nationally in the banking and property world.

Edwards himself was a factory man: his clients built them, funded them and in many cases worked in them. Edwards loved factories. They made goods that a country could sell. Factories for Edwards were the real backbone of the English economy: they provided real jobs and created real wealth. Until his involvement with W. Moorcroft Plc, it had been a matter of serious regret that he might finish his legal career as a champion paper pusher, a maker of money for his clients with little more to the sum total of his life than a mountain of pretentious words for which he had been paid and which were, in turn, quickly forgotten.

John Rainford had been a good friend of the Edwards family. It was John who had offered Hugh the job with Richards Butler in 1966, and John's wife, Sheila, was godmother to Karen, one of Hugh and Maureen's daughters. Without Rainford's guidance, Hugh's career at Richards Butler might well have been different. Soon after the announcement of his retirement, John had stood down from his role as Head of Department, and Edwards had been elected to take his place by the other partners in the Property Group.

At this point, Edwards was forced to take stock of his position. One human being could do only so much. In effect, he now became involved in running a leading international law firm, heading up one of its departments, and, additionally, was one of only four people managing one of the world's leading art potteries. By a process of careful delegation Edwards decided that he could cope, but the departure of the Moorcroft design team had come at a particularly difficult time for him. The appointment of a new full-time designer was not just a priority, it was also an obsession.

Edwards had consulted with his Partners at Richards Butler, and it had been agreed that Moorcroft would make something unique to celebrate John Rainford's retirement. Maureen was delighted. John and Gill were agreeable, and Edwards tackled Rachel Bishop on the subject shortly thereafter. Rachel had completed her revised design of the Special Occasions White Rose vase for 1993, and the consensus was that it was good. Pansies, however, had yet again proved just how difficult they were as a flower to work up into a design. Rachel had complained that they 'died', that they were without grace and uninspiring, that they lacked life, and whatever way they were treated the result was always the same.

Dull, boring and flat! At the moment Edwards raised the subject of the John Rainford presentation piece, Rachel had just taken Pansies to another starting point. She would try and make them 'young', injecting some life into the structure of the design through the base colour mix of the vase. Edwards shuddered. It took little imagination to see Justin Emery shaking with silent rage.

Apart from the law, there were three loves in John Rainford's life: his wife and children, early English silver spoons and Shakespeare. Few people could have seen more Shakespeare at the Barbican than John and Sheila Rainford, and of all Shakespeare's plays the Rainford favourite was 'A Midsummer Night's Dream'. This suggested a starting point for a design theme. More importantly, it gave Rachel the degree of design freedom which Moorcroft had been unable to offer up to that moment. Wild flowers had featured heavily in her original interview portfolio, and for the first time her eyes flashed in a way which showed that she now had a challenge worthy of pursuit.

White Rose: 1993 Special Occasions vase. Height 5"

She had, she casually announced, already given notice to her present employers to concentrate on her Moorcroft commissions. Edwards pointed out that those commissions apart, Rachel would have no work from the end of that month. When she had broken the news to him, Edwards had studied her carefully. Leaving her job was not simply a ploy to become the new Moorcroft designer, he was sure of that. This was a positive act from a determined and ambitious young woman. Rachel would now be able to give herself all the time and concentration required to design properly and experiment freely. Without that freedom Rachel had no chance of achieving the standards required of her, and the Moorcroft design job would never be hers. Edwards had always admired the courage in people who had conviction in their own ability and were prepared to make sacrifices to prove it; at the same time, he found it difficult not to display a withering contempt for people who thought they were more significant than they really were.

One week later, at Rachel's request, Edwards was reading the text of a speech by King Oberon from 'A Midsummer Night's Dream' which Rachel had identified for use as inspiration for her design for a Moorcroft Charger:

I know a bank where the wild thyme blows
Where oxlips and the nodding violet grows
Quite over-canopied with luscious woodbine
With sweet musk-roses and with eglantine....

The choice was perfect; the quotation would be written onto the base of the charger and fired in under the glaze. Rachel's design incorporated all the flowers mentioned by King Oberon, and the first watercolour was a balance of well-structured design and simple, rich colours. The trial piece was painted by leading paintress, Wendy Mason, and the result not far short of pure magic. John Moorcroft's silence spoke volumes, but for Edwards the anxieties of the past three months evaporated like morning mist.

The Oberon charger was the essence of Moorcroft right down to its last tube-lined curve and colour blend; the colours played with each other; it was a merry-go-round of design perfection. Colour, shape and tube-lining all played their part. Gill had remarked that it was a pity for the design to be used on only one piece – she backed away from the word 'waste'. Maureen was adamant; other than the two existing trials, no Oberon charger would ever again be made. The Edwards owed that to John and Sheila Rainford. As a concession to collectors, and at Gill's request, it was agreed that Rachel's original watercolour drawing of the Rainford Charger would be used as a limited edition print. Apart from the two prototypes themselves, slight deviants on the chosen colourway, the presentation piece would remain forever unique.

The Moorcrofts and the Edwards now understood two important facts. The first was that Rachel Bishop had crossed the bridge. She was not just a competent ceramics designer: she had the capacity to take her art, in the Moorcroft idiom, onto an altogether higher plane. The second fact flowed swiftly from the first. A way had to be found to introduce Oberon as a range in January 1994, without diminishing the rarity and significance of the John Rainford charger.

All four of the Moorcroft Board were confident in their belief that Oberon would appeal to Moorcroft collectors all over the world, and that time would prove it to be one of the great Moorcroft designs. For Edwards there was a more worrying implication. If Rachel's success had sprung from her brave decision not to run two jobs, which of his own two jobs should be pushed to the sideline? His wife quickly identified herself with that particular conundrum, pointing out to her husband that she had already decided to give up her own law practice to concentrate on

Moorcroft – despite the conclusion of her most successful year ever as a solicitor. It was not yet time, they decided, for two people in the same family to make the same sacrifice. By the time the Moorcroft centenary year arrived in 1997, Edwards would be fifty-five, and at that age he could take honourable retirement from Richards Butler if he wanted to, and still preserve the goodwill of his Partners.

SEVEN

No Room at the Works

It was one of Justin Emery's more endearing characteristics that he refused to accept the fact that an increased demand for Moorcroft around the world would inevitably create a corresponding need for more tube-liners and decorators. Hugh Edwards had never been entirely sure whether this reluctance sprang from an inner disbelief that people could really want to have an expensive piece of art pottery in their homes to enjoy or whether increased demand, in Justin's book of rules, could result only from activity in the field of cheap 'fancies' which were a speciality of the Stoke-on-Trent pottery industry in which Justin had been schooled. Either way, throughout the early nineties the Moorcroft Works Manager would occasionally hit his production head painfully on the ceiling of a shortage of skilled staff. Moorcroft decorators and tube-liners took up to a year to train, and the procedures necessary to increase capacity were slow as a result.

The crisis specifically exercising the Moorcroft Board's collective mind had begun to rear its head towards the end of 1992, even before there had been any inkling that the design team would leave. Put simply, there was no more room at the Works to seat and train new tube-liners or decorators, even if suitable people could be recruited. The Moorcroft bottle kiln is a Grade II listed building of outstanding architectural and historic importance, and the Local Planning Authority would inevitably scrutinise very closely any planning application for an extension to the Works which might detract from the overall appearance of the Moorcroft buildings. The consensus was that Hugh Edwards, whose activities as a solicitor had more than once given him an opportunity of negotiating with the City Planning Officer in Stoke-on-Trent, should seek the Planning Permission and the Listed Building Consent that were both required before an extension could be built.

FACING: *Painters and tube-liners at work in the refurbished decorating shop.*

Edwards instructed Hulme Upright and Partners, a good local firm of architects in Stoke-on-Trent with a wide and sensitive experience in Listed Building work. Past work with Hulme Upright's David Carr on similar projects would, he felt, stand him in good stead. John Sambrook, another Partner in the same firm, joined the team, and the planning applications were prepared although not formally lodged. The view was that a process of discussion was more likely to produce the required result than the combative approach so loved by many planning experts.

Throughout, Edwards was forced to admit that the Chief Planning Officer's department had been extremely constructive. A number of sensible modifications were suggested and included in the scheme. As a result, the fine balance between a desire to create new jobs on the one hand and the need to protect the spirit and integrity of the original building on the other was successfully maintained. In February 1993, Stoke-on-Trent City Council issued planning permission, and four days later Edwards signed a building contract with Clive Plant Limited after competitive tender. By March the contractors had started work on site, and the first material Moorcroft factory extension for more than sixty years was underway.

In essence, the scheme was simple. The old Works canteen would be demolished, and on the cleared site, as an integral part of the Works, a new two-storey building would be constructed. On the first floor a new, modern Works canteen would be sited, larger and more light and airy than its predecessor. Included in the plans for the ground floor was a new ladies' toilet block, not to mention new administrative offices and extra design space for Rachel. With the additional administrative space in place, it would then be possible to dismantle the former office area in the middle of the factory, merging that space with the old decorating shop, thus increasing the size of the latter by thirty per cent in the process. For the Moorcroft Board the result was exceptionally rewarding, and by June 1993 additional decorators and tube-liners had been recruited to start training in the enlarged decorating shop.

Anxious as always to secure the best possible working conditions for those at Moorcroft, the Works Manager had insisted that the process of mixing Moorcroft's metallic oxide colours be taken out of the decorating shop and placed in its own controlled space alongside. The packing and dispatch area was opened up to make it light and airy, and a new inner wall and floor were put in place to remove from the packing shed all traces of dampness caused by rain driven onto the western flank wall of the factory built with bricks made in 1911.

Justin Emery was especially proud of the new packing and dispatch area, with its new men's toilet block. In 1986 the men's toilet had been open to the stars, while the latest model even sported a hot-air hand dryer as well as trendy pink and purple tiles from floor to ceiling. The new disabled toilet opposite matched in every feature. Walter Moorcroft writing in the December 1993 Collectors' Newsletter commented:

Nostalgia, in all its forms, has to be kept in perspective and its best feature is to actually highlight the improvements which have taken place in our conditions of working and living. It is more than gratifying to see that the efforts of the last eighty years have been completed during the course of this year by the restructuring of the factory to a standard fit for the 21st Century.

Any change in a familiar building inevitably results in a shock to the system. John had known the Works man and boy, and had been part of the team for more than thirty years. On the day after the Wakes Holidays in July 1993, Edwards had telephoned to enquire about two retailers trying to jump the production schedule, a form of commercial cheating which reputable manufacturers frown upon. John, he thought, sounded distant and uneasy. Gentle enquiry established that John felt disorientated. Familiar features had disappeared, including the office in which he had worked for more than twenty years.

Edwards' own exposure to Moorcroft had been a modest seven years. Even so, his first sight of the completed project gave him a severe jolt. The old offices had vanished, and the enlarged decorating shop seemed unbelievably big – a feeling, Edwards later discovered, shared by most of those who worked in it. There were, however, two real and enormous gains. First, there was now a logical and circular production route from the clay shop and 'turning' area to the decorating shop, and from there to the dipping area and kilns. The second advantage flowed from the first. Visitors could enjoy a tour of the Works unfolding in sequence.

More strangely, the whole decorating shop almost glowed in the clear light that filtered through the new north-facing roof lights and the large windows which had been a feature of the decorating shop for decades. Edwards decided that William Morris would have approved. The extension had given Moorcroft a one-off opportunity to create a good and safe working environment for both staff and management alike. All work should be enjoyable or it is not worth doing at all. An unpleasant work place is no better than a prison, a place to which people are obliged to come and to earn enough money to live. If work is to be enjoyed, a pleasant working environment is an essential ingredient.

John Moorcroft's morning greeting

Another important component is the right of a person to share in the fruits of his or her own labour. From the early 1990's, after Moorcroft had moved back into profit, the company operated a system under which its profits had been shared out among all those who worked there. All that was now required, Edwards had decided, was to devise a scheme whereby the Moorcroft employees could lawfully receive their profit tax free; but such a scheme would take time to work out. It had been the Moorcroft auditors who had pointed out that in the year ending 31 July 1993, profit payments had been made to all staff for the first time at a level which exceeded the percentage paid to shareholders in the same year! That fact alone justified the investment of part of Edwards' ever-diminishing free time in devising a tax saving scheme which worked for the Moorcroft corporate family. Eventually it was done, and by 1 August 1994, the Moorcroft profit-related pay scheme was in operation after formal approval from the Inland Revenue a week earlier.

William Morris would have approved of the profit-sharing philosophy, too, but the army of corporate performance watchers in the City of London would not – unless, of course, it was a scheme for them to enjoy themselves. Edwards had a deep-rooted hatred of the men with computer screens: the go-go dealers and analysts who told you that your corporate performance had fallen by two percentage points in the preceding month. True wealth was something you made with your hands and could hold in your hands: something which gave real pleasure to the maker, the purchaser and the retailer who took it into stock. One day, staff might be persuaded to take shares in the company as well as profit; but traditions die hard in the potteries where in some cases directors still have their own toilets and staff have been taught over generations to 'know their place'.

EIGHT

Open Season, Open Weekend

John Moorcroft had felt sorry for Clive Plant Limited, the contractors appointed to build the new factory extension. This arose from the fact that the contractor had twice been the victim of particularly mean thefts from the premises during the construction period. On the first occasion, all tools and machinery left lying around after the factory gates closed had been stolen. On the second, thieves had broken the site hut window to gain access, taking everything they could lay their hands on. In the event the contractor still delivered 'on time', which had enabled John to quip that Stoke-on-Trent builders did not need penalty clauses to make them perform! Sadly, however, the contractor's experience had only mirrored Moorcroft's own similar misfortunes over a period of more than two years.

Traditionalists would have said that the unmodernised Moorcroft factory had 'character'. In the past this meant that rain fell through holes in the roof; liquid slip was carried around in heavy plastic watering cans; and visitors to the factory shop would trip after catching their heels in uneven old brickwork on the floor. It also made it easy for thieves to bludgeon their crude way into the Works after axing out Moorcroft's old wooden doors. Charm and character cannot withstand sledgehammers and iron bars. It had been Moorcroft's misfortune to have been burgled five times in the period from January 1991 to August 1993, and this took no account of the losses suffered by the building contractors.

The old wooden doors, inside the Works and outside, soon became a thing of the past. In their place appeared strong doors lined with steel and hung on steel frames. Even the frames were bolted hard to the brick and concrete fabric of the Works. A complex and sensitive system of alarms now guarded the premises at all times. Television cameras relentlessly scanned factory shop and museum, while Group 4 signs hung on the perimeter fence reflected their continual vigilance. The perimeter fence itself, eight feet high with a cranked, barbed wire head, could set off reactions that would deliver the police to the Works in what seemed only seconds.

All this caused John Moorcroft great sadness mixed with anger and concern. The savage recession of the first years of the 1990's had witnessed, perversely, unprecedented growth in the popularity of Moorcroft pottery. By the end of 1993, staffing levels were back to those of the company's heyday in the mid-1920's, but with success came the thieves. It cost the company a great deal of money to keep them out – as much as 10 pence on each piece Moorcroft Pottery produced, Edwards had once calculated. For both the Moorcrofts and the Edwards, success was tinged with unhappiness that some stolen pieces of good pottery were finding their way into car boot sales and some less-than-reputable dealers, auction houses and antique fairs. It had been a sobering experience to sit in front of a television set watching a video recording of a door being broken down and hooded thieves lifting art pottery from stock shelves or a gang of shoplifters slithering round a crowd of customers in the factory shop to fill their bags and pockets.

Security at the Moorcroft factory had been designated as John's responsibility. As a result, he tended to construe each break-in as a mark of failure and each failed attempt as a mark of success. In 1993 there seemed to be more excitement about Open Weekend than ever before, but the prospect of more than five hundred people swarming all over the Works filled John with alarm. Gill's organisation was thorough. John could not recall an occasion when this had not been the case, but at the end of the day security was still his problem. All reasonable precautions to deter thieves had been put in place.

The morning of 5 June 1993 dawned sunny and fine. There were no problems with the two talks at Stoke City Museum and Art Gallery. David Battie of Sotheby's, although only recently recovered from a nasty bout of pneumonia, was in his best 'Antiques Roadshow' form and delighted the assembled collectors with a skilled and often humorous presentation. It was a delivery which both reflected and honoured the past.

The Board had decided that Hugh Edwards would give the second talk, and for him, as always, the subject had to reflect his drive and single-minded ambition to keep Moorcroft moving forward. During the preceding week John and Gill had spontaneously suggested that Rachel's position as freelance designer should be reviewed. The post of Designer was still open, and the mood of both families was that it should be filled. The result was a short but momentous Board meeting held during the evening of 4 June, the day before Open Weekend.

In the space of ten minutes the Moorcroft Board unanimously resolved to appoint Rachel Joanne Bishop as only the fourth full-time designer of the company in almost one hundred years. Rachel agreed to accept the appointment. With the decision recorded in the Moorcroft Minute Book, Hugh used his Open Day talk to tell the assembled collectors about the qualities required of a Moorcroft designer: a sense of history and a sense of humour, consummate skill in the Moorcroft idiom, an unbreakable determination to overcome all obstacles, a sensitive understanding of the life of a Works Manager, a close rapport on clearly defined terms with the decorating staff at the factory and the strength of purpose to resist all attempts to influence the direction of the designer's art.

It was a comfort for Edwards to recall that William Moorcroft had been appointed as designer to James Macintyre & Co. Ltd. in 1897 at the age of 24 years, precisely the same age that Rachel Bishop had been on that momentous

Left: 'Tiffany' by Wendy Mason. Height 12"
Right: 'Brittany' by Beverley Wilkes. Height 12"

Friday in June. Youth and energy were qualities to be prized and not spurned. You could, John commented later, have heard a pin drop in the lecture theatre at Stoke City Museum, so intense was the concentration of the Moorcroft collectors who watched history unfold before their eyes. Never one to resist the temptation of a dramatic presentation, Edwards had asked John to join him on stage. From his lecture notes he produced the first prototype of Rachel's contract of employment, and with warm supportive applause from the audience, Rachel came forward to receive the draft contract as the symbol of her appointment from John Moorcroft, the younger son of the founding father. A new era in Moorcroft design had begun.

The collectors who wound their way through the streets of Stoke-on-Trent that weekend, had an unusual target for their enthusiasm back at the Works. Not only had some of the surplus pieces from the Moorcroft Museum collection been put out for sale, but also Peter Blood's auction was known to contain offerings altogether different from anything that had gone under the hammer in previous years. The Moorcroft decorators were looking for a different approach to their annual contribution to the Collectors' Club Auction. From the time Richard and Sally Dennis had been in charge of design, the Moorcroft Board permitted them only to take an existing design of the company and colour it up in a colourway of their own choice. The pieces that resulted were then auctioned – identical pieces in each colourway offered on each of the two open days.

It was that part of the proceedings which the Moorcroft decorators wanted to change, although the other part, the destination of the proceeds of sale from the auction, they did not! The proceeds of sale were 'pooled', and the pool, after deduction of income tax and national insurance, was divided among all staff at the factory. Now the decorators wanted to design as well as decorate their own pieces, and for the first time the Moorcroft Board felt able to agree. The decorating shop divided itself into teams. Each team chose a designer, and when the design work was complete each member of the team decorated one piece for each day of the Open Weekend in a colourway of their own personal choice.

The Auctioneer's hammer can be a cruel judge of quality, but any residual Board anxiety at the wisdom of their decision was quickly dispelled. Peter Blood was soon knocking down prices at levels which caused a number of eyebrows to rise. Beverley Wilkes' Brittany was a star turn in the designer's own chosen colourway, securing a price in excess of £800, whilst Wendy Mason's Tiffany was not far behind – and with it a silhouette of the first Moorcroft nude! A combination of the pieces designed by the Moorcroft staff and a sparkling performance by Peter Blood on the auctioneer's rostrum caused the auction contribution to the Moorcroft staff payout almost to double the total of the previous year. Edwards was happy, too. If there was a designer in the decorating shop waiting to be seen, it was best to know of the fact.

Also on offer during those two, hectic June days were the first Rachel Bishop butterfly vases, later to be seen as heralds of things to come. Designed specially for Open Weekend on the popular 32/5″ shape with an ivory ground, those on offer were soon only to be seen wrapped in tissue paper and packed for their journey to a new home. Collectors who were not fortunate enough to attend Open Weekend were given the opportunity to buy up the residue of one hundred and twenty-five unnumbered pieces.

It was a memorable weekend for John Moorcroft, who was also greatly relieved to see it pass. There had been no thefts, no break-ins, and as Justin Emery had remarked with something approaching a smile, no breakages. Collectors had signalled their approval to the appointment of Rachel Bishop as Designer, and Moorcroft management could once again concentrate on the serious business of making Moorcroft pottery.

1993 Collectors' Club Open Day butterfly vase. Height 5"

NINE

From Pansies to Kyoto

Maureen Edwards had never much liked pansies as a flower. Like John, she felt that they lacked synergy with any other flower, a fact she found irritating. For any kind of flower display they were almost worse than useless. That Rachel had struggled with her task to design a range of pansies caused her no surprise. Although the suggestion that pansies should be reintroduced had now rumbled around for more than a year, nothing had been achieved. Delay could not hide the fact that pansies were flowers for painters to demonstrate their skills rather than tube-liners. Their broad, colourful petals offered a challenge to a good painter, in contrast to the heavily tube-lined pottery which Moorcroft had introduced over recent years, and which in turn had left little to challenge the painter's art. More significantly, the painters were restless about occasional enforced idleness at a time when Moorcroft was bursting at the seams with new orders – and their rumbles of discontent were audible. Against this background, a 'painting piece' continued to be an essential design and production objective, and it was the designer who had to perform first.

Rachel's protests that pansies just died on her met with sympathy, but the 'press on' philosophy prevailed. Less stout hearts would have given up and gone away. More than once, Rachel was forced to retrace her steps and start again – muttering darkly about flowers that were suitable only for funerals. William Moorcoft, she once reminded Maureen, had only three colours available for pansies – blue/purple, cream and maroon – while the current Thompson and Morgan seed catalogue offered dozens of different colours, shapes and sizes. Pansies in the intervening seventy years had come a long way, and bore little resemblance to the Viola Tricolor or Heartsease much loved by Shakespeare.

Several weeks of untold frustration centred around a design involving a flower

FACING: *Pansy drawing, trial plate and vase and ((top right) vase from the final range: Height 8″*

Pansy group: Diameter of bowl 8″, tallest vase 6″

which Rachel would have preferred not to have used in the first place. That frustration caused her to revert to her own instincts, creating a design with a colour combination more easily identified with youth than old age. The result somewhat stunned the Board, but objection might have forced them to admit to an average age of fifty-plus. Only a week before 1993's Open Weekend, Rachel's Pansy range received design approval with little comment other than a visible display of genuine relief all round. The use of coral, purple and pink on a rouge ground was not what the Moorcroft directors had had in mind, but universal praise from all of their children carried the day.

Any residual doubts that might have lingered were quickly dispelled at an international trade fair held at Birmingham's National Exhibition Centre in July. Rachel Bishop's Pansy range constituted 47% of the total sales. During the following months until the Moorcroft sales team were instructed to 'down sell' to avoid a production crisis, Pansies were well on their way to becoming a best-selling range.

In one of Rachel Bishop's early conversations with Hugh, the two of them had reached a consensus on design with a story attached, particularly if that story had the art historians scurrying for their notebooks. During the previous year the Edwards had travelled to Japan with the Dennises for a Moorcroft sales exhibition and had satisfied a lifelong ambition to visit the ancient city of Kyoto, until 1868 the imperial capital of Japan. Much of what the two Moorcroft enthusiasts saw might well have been useful had they been designers. One sight especially stood out far beyond all others, to which not even the Golden Pavilion could hold a torch. The main gate to the Emperor's Palace in Kyoto was absolutely classic in terms of Japanese line and dimension, its great wooden timbers still supporting a roof which reflected centuries of toil. This ancient gate stopped the Edwards dead in their tracks, and the family camera was put to good use.

It was, however, the underside of the gate roof which provoked the greatest attention. Intricately carved wood and delicately painted designs depicted images that might have been lifted directly from William De Morgan's studio a hundred years earlier. There was only one problem. The Kyoto images predated William De Morgan by almost five hundred years. Dragons, butterflies, scrolling foliage, cranes in flight and flowers in full bloom all came together in the underside of that magnificent gateway. Hugh finished his film, wondering at the same time if De Morgan had sat under that very same gate to copy the designs onto his sketch pad. The impact was enormous; history and art sitting together for artistic philistines like themselves to enjoy generation after generation. The Edwards returned from Japan with a mission. Somehow the Kyoto images had to be interpreted into the Moorcroft idiom for Moorcroft collectors to enjoy and appreciate.

It was the photographic experts who first had to work their skills. Maureen spent a considerable period of time closeted with commercial photographers in Saffron Walden. The photographers subjected the Kyoto photographs to intense scrutiny, each possible area of interest massively enlarged until the total scope of the medieval images caught by the camera lens could be seen. There were revelations at every stage. Scenes of ancient mythology, emperors riding dragons, strange flowers, insects and birds, each with its own section and each telling its own story. It was a design feast of a kind the Moorcroft Board had never seen before, and as soon as she saw the enlarged detail Rachel needed no further prompting or encouragement to move in on it. Within two weeks of Open Weekend, mould-maker Trevor Critchlow was wrestling with a new vase of huge proportions which Rachel had drawn in profile. Kyoto was on the move, and the Kyoto vase was to be the Moorcroft flagship at the International Spring Fair at Birmingham in 1994. No one was in any doubt about that.

The amount of time Maureen had spent with the photographers over what were to become known in Moorcroft folklore as the Kyoto weeks had prompted a further and more vigorous resurgence of anxiety concerning the Moorcroft centenary year in Hugh's mind. The first of January 1997 would arrive in a rush with Arts and Crafts appetites already whetted by the centenary of William Morris the year before – not to mention a strong resurgence of interest in Charles Rennie Mackintosh, the Glasgow artist, designer and architect in the same year. No serious discussions had taken place on how Moorcroft should celebrate the William Morris centenary, and that fact on its own was a serious omission. So, too, was the Moorcroft failure to take note of the great Mackintosh exhibition, scheduled to

Pansy group: Plate diameter 10″, tallest vase 7″

open in Glasgow in Spring 1996 and thereafter moving to New York, Chicago and Los Angeles. Even so, Hugh felt obliged to push both thoughts to the back of his mind and to concentrate on more pressing matters concerning Moorcroft's own centenary.

Hugh's friendship with Michael Bruce, the well-known photographer and collector of old Moorcroft, stretched back over a number of years. Michael's skilled rescue operation of the famous Victorian glass photographic plates discovered by the Moorcrofts in the garage of John's mother's house in Albert Road, Trentham, had made a particularly important contribution to the preservation of Moorcroft history. Almost a century old, the plates had been carefully stabilized and lovingly preserved. Good prints and enlargements had been taken to establish the detailed features of these vases at the time of publication of Paul Atterbury's book, *Moorcroft*. The series of enlargements which Michael Bruce produced had caused great excitement. As far as anyone knew, one of the vases caught by the camera lens a century earlier had never been found from the day the original had been photographed. To find that original vase decorated with yachts would be a collector's dream, but with each year that passed the chances of that dream becoming a reality inevitably became less and less.

It would almost be nice, Edwards had mused to himself, if an example of the Florian yacht vase failed to come to light before the onset of Moorcroft's centenary year. Under such circumstances, it would be quite legitimate for Moorcroft to make the vase as a centenary piece, designed as it had been by the founding father of Moorcroft pottery. The Moorcroft Board had agreed with him in principle; but once decisions were made, Edwards never stood still. It was not in his nature. While the others were still analysing the Kyoto photographs, Edwards had moved on and was studying the old Florian yacht prints under his magnifying glass. Michael Bruce might even have been right when he said that there were people on the yachts! The detail would be difficult for both tube-liners and decorators. This fact alone suggested that the Moorcroft Works Manager would have an almighty fit and almost certainly fight the creation of the Florian yacht vase on the ground that if no pieces had survived, a previous Works Manager at James Macintyre & Co had probably rejected it and broken the prototype a hundred years earlier!

FACING: *Kyoto vase: Height 24"*

TEN

Design Explosion

Early in 1993, a strategic decision had been made to sell Moorcroft pottery directly into Canada rather than through the medium of a national agent or distributor. Long-term relationships with overseas distributors are difficult to forge and take a long time to develop.

Canada had always been a special and enthusiastic market for Moorcroft. In 1990 David Simmonds had decided that to distribute Moorcroft as well as run his own property development business and furniture factory were too much for one man to handle. A friend to the last, he organised a fresh distribution network through Frederick Dickson. Dicksons had been known to John for some years, and John was comfortable with the change. The Collectors' Club continued to be professionally administered locally by David Simmonds, a role he was to perform with skill and integrity right through to Moorcroft's centenary year.

Moorcroft pottery had been exported to Canada since the early years of the century and the post-war era from 1945 to 1970 had been particularly vigorous. To John's regret, Dicksons gave up the Moorcroft distributorship only two years later. Sales in Canada had been stagnant for some time, and the world recession had hit the Canadian economy particularly hard, even though elsewhere in the world demand for Moorcroft was rising sharply. To deal with the Canadian problem, and at his request, John was given responsibility for opening up the market by direct selling. Although his first trip in March 1993 was a gruelling one, it had also been a success.

In the space of ten days John covered seven thousand miles and visited no fewer than eleven stores. With that level of resource committed to Canada, the Moorcroft Board had felt it only right to make a similar effort on behalf of Keith Lippert, Moorcroft's sole distributor in the United States. So in October 1993, John made a promotional trip to America, visited twelve stores and during the visit travelled another six thousand miles as ambassador for his family name. With a major

FACING: *Oberon, detail*

promotion in Australia and New Zealand scheduled for 1994, the demands made by the export market on John's time were considerable.

In an ideal world, catalogues and samples for the New Year are dispatched abroad to arrive in their country of destination well before Christmas. When this objective is achieved, it gives Moorcroft's overseas agents and distributors an opportunity to order and take into stock new designs before the main European trade shows take place in January and February. In turn, the old Moorcroft theory continued, overseas orders arriving over the Christmas period gives the factory an opportunity to work on new designs during December, January and February, traditionally the quiet quarter in the ceramics industry.

Until 1993, this theory had proved difficult to put into practice for a variety of reasons. To produce and photograph new designs in time to dispatch catalogues and catch the export market early meant that the prototypes of new pieces, across all ranges, have to be ready before the middle of October. John was determined that for 1994, catalogues and samples would be dispatched overseas in good time – and 'in good time' meant during the first week of December at the latest. Rachel's already proven capacity for hard work had made it likely that the 1994 catalogue would include the prestige vase used to front up the display on the Moorcroft stand at the Birmingham Spring Fair in February. The mighty Kyoto vase had seen to that. Pansies, too, were at last ready for the 1994 catalogue following their successful launch three months earlier, although some new shapes had been added to the range in response to collector demand.

Of other new ranges, there was precious little evidence. As a result, John's annual fear of late

Groups of Butterfly range: tall vase 10″

FACING: *Three groups of pieces and a vase from the Oberon collection: single vase 10″*

catalogue delivery had once more begun to manifest itself. In his mind there lurked a strong personal wish to have something new to talk about. A good manufacturer always knows that he can only please retail customers and collectors alike with new shapes and designs which can be both made and delivered on time.

Throughout the summer of 1993, Rachel had been burning the midnight oil seven nights a week in the Moorcroft design studio. Good artists were like that Edwards had commented, and those long, irregular hours in Stoke-on-Trent had been followed, more often than not, by a week's 'green fix' somewhere in the open countryside to recover. One of Rachel's 'green fixes' had been taken in the New Forest, out of which had sprung a complete range of ivory pots decorated with butterflies. First time round, a number of pieces in her proposed range had been rejected. Protests from Gill and Maureen included reference to long strands of unbroken green tube-lining across a white surface. To decorate a Moorcroft pot in this way carried with it a risk of tube-line damage in much the same way as the original

A group of Foxglove vases: tall vase 14″

design team's Fuchsia prototype had done two years earlier with its novel use of red tube-lining. However, before the Board had even had time to meet again, Rachel produced revised prototype designs of her butterfly vases – all of which neatly eliminated the potential tube-lining problem.

Almost miraculously, it seemed to John, September saw three new William Morris Golden Lily pieces emerge from the glost kiln. John had not been aware that Rachel was a professed disciple of William Morris, in the same way that he had not been aware any change in the Golden Lily presentation was possible. The Moorcrofts and the Edwards had been schooled in the doctrine of perfection preached by the previous design team that Golden Lily would translate only onto

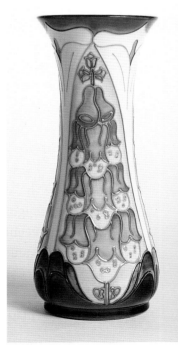

Foxglove vase: Height 12″

the 393/12″ vase. Indeed, it had taken a great deal of effort by John to persuade the design team even to translate the design onto a charger. For this reason he was surprised to see the three new Golden Lily pieces which Rachel introduced to the Board for approval. Gill was content to say that it would be nice to be able to offer smaller pieces in a lower price bracket than hitherto. Hugh remained silent. A modest extension to the Golden Lily range would be nothing like enough to persuade the public to buy William Morris pieces during the artist poet's centenary year, and he knew it.

Much as the Board had anticipated the Oberon design seemed to fall onto every shape selected for production, and each new piece caused as much instant excitement in the Works as its predecessor. Even the tea set, despite its cost, was generally accepted as the finest of its kind, in design terms, produced by Moorcroft in the recent past. The flowers seemed to dance with each other; the colours faded from one colour tone to another as if joined forever. The chemistry was exact, and even Justin Emery was as near to happiness as a Works Manager could ever be about a new design. A subtle touch of coral added to the plain grey band on each piece created an overall appeal which would be especially appreciated by Moorcroft collectors. Trialling was complete. To launch a new design with nineteen pieces was without precedent, and the colour impact of the range was as stunning as it was new.

At the other end of the scale, sales figures for Buttercup suggested that the time had come to discontinue that range, and this message had been relayed to Rachel the previous June. There had been rumours circulating around the factory that drawings showing Foxgloves framed by large white lilies

William Morris Golden Lily designs in two colour ways – all discontinued in 1995 except the 10″ ivory vase, below right. Tall vase 12″.

Trellis clock

had been seen. Large white lilies smacked of a skilled tube-lining input, and a widespread unease developed that Foxglove would remove the co-operative smile from the Works Manager's face, as well as the more relaxed attitudes that had developed over recent weeks in the tube-lining section. At this point, however, everything seemed to happen at once. Foxglove vases popped up all over the Works, mixed in with the redesigned Butterfly vases.

John was delighted. An early launch of the 1994 catalogue was still a real possibility – until, that was, Hypericum appeared. Rachel had taken into account the pending demise of Buttercup and had decided that good catalogue balance required a replacement from the yellow/blue stable of Moorcroft's repertoire of colours. Edwards had a suspicion that Rachel's unusually good rapport with the Works Manager had something to do with the smooth arrival of Hypericum, which had been liked immediately by all those who saw it, and particularly by Justin Emery. Decorated onto a celadon body, the simple flowing lines were brought to life by a magical blue tint on the white, tube-lined stamens of the flowers – a colour, some had remarked, not unlike the blue seen in a brandy flame. The 7″ jug, Gill Moorcroft commented, was an exceptionally attractive piece. For John the range had 'traditional' appeal, and for that reason he abandoned his initial reservations and offered the new range his full support.

At this moment the whole process of design became enjoyable and alive. The vibrant impact of Oberon, the rich warmth of Foxglove, the coolness of Hypericum and the gentleness of Butterflies together made the prospects for 1994 exciting. For good measure, and again with the Works Manager's co-operation, a clock decorated with climbing flowers on a trellis to be produced in an edition limited to 250 pieces was added to the list at Rachel's request. In point of fact, Justin Emery had been quietly fuming about the Foxglove pieces. His patience had already been sorely tested with the simultaneous arrival of the 1994 year plate decorated with a Peacock; but he failed to explode.

In turn, John was able to supervise Harold Bowen's photography in accordance with his own cherished timetable. The 1994 catalogue went to press, and before

FACING: *Pots from the Hypericum range – discontinued 1995*

the year ended export orders were arriving in the post, through the fax machine and over the telephone. Although Moorcroft had introduced more new designs in 1987, no single Moorcroft designer had ever produced as many new designs on as many new shapes as Rachel Bishop introduced to the world in 1994. The design presentation was complete, and the impact immediate and dramatic. By the end of the spring trade fair season, 1994's new designs were outselling the old in a ratio of six to two, and incoming orders leaped by a massive 140% over the same period in the preceding year.

Just occasionally, Edwards had to remind himself, making art pottery was a business, and to succeed you needed both to design and deliver top quality ware on time. Fiddling around did not pay wages, settle Moorcroft's huge electricity bills or fund the expansion and modernisation necessary to create a decent working environment for all those involved in making Moorcroft pottery. The salesmen now had even more to sell. Everything was in place to service the demand for Moorcroft provoked by its new and hitherto unknown designer. All in all, Edwards had remarked to his wife, 1993 had proved to be an excellent year, and 1994 was not only underway but also under control.

1994 Peacock plate

ELEVEN

Horse Sense

Just how the 7/5″ Heartsease Special Occasions vase came into existence was something of a mystery to the Edwards. There was a touch of the 'geometrics' in the design and the colours were traditional, simple and chemically compatible. When Hugh intimated that he liked the piece, John Moorcroft had looked mildly pleased. There was a logic, John had remarked offhandedly, that after Pansies and the use of Viola Tricolor in Oberon, the wild pansy itself should command individual attention. The pot had photographed well, and the Moorcroft Board had no difficulty in approving the design for production. John's logic turned out to be prophetically accurate. Although 1994 included an extended tour of Australia for John, fractionally under a thousand Heartsease pieces were sold. In so doing, this Special Occasions vase outsold by a wide margin all its predecessors, including Rachel Bishop's own White Rose Special Occasions vase launched in 1993.

John was comfortable with Heartsease, and when you are in the business of promotion and selling it is critical that the seller feels comfortable. Maureen Edwards had commented during the 1994 Spring Fair at Birmingham that a salesman could sell anything that he liked – literally. Put another way, there is always an inherent danger that the act of selling reflects only the seller's point of view – dangerous in the world of art pottery. Art pottery should not require selling; it should invite selection. The seller should be ready with enthusiastic responses to the buyer's taste and cultural preferences.

Whenever John felt comfortable, it enabled him to respond enthusiastically to potential buyers who sought his approval of their purchases. As Maureen had pointed out, if a salesman 'sold' his personal taste to a retail customer, the retailer's success with a potential collector could well be influenced by the salesman's own taste – or lack of it. Occasionally a design not much liked by a salesman would move only slowly in the early part of the year following its launch. If orders from retailers then began to accelerate, the only conclusion to be drawn was that the salesman's taste was not synonymous with those most important of all people, the ultimate purchasers. Conversely a sensitive salesman quickly learns when a design is not being well received or has outlived its natural shelf-life.

Introduction of date marks by Moorcroft in 1990, largely on the initiative of Richard Dennis, had done a great deal to help collectors and discourage dishonest dealers. The date mark for each year would always tell a collector the year in which the piece was made. Overnight, it had become difficult to sell an Anemone Blue design as being 'late 1930s' to an unsuspecting victim, when an arrow on the base indicated quite clearly that the piece had been made in 1990. This indication was seldom a matter of importance to a retailer, but it sometimes reflected the fact, proved often during almost a hundred years of Moorcroft history, that a design was dying and was ready for discontinuation. By July 1994, Rainforest, Finches Teal and Red Tulip were already looking frail, and demand for Mamoura had fallen as well. It was too soon to start considering discontinuation for 1995, but the message coming back from Moorcroft salesmen Alan Wright and Steven Swann suggested those ranges were ready to disappear. Alan and Steven were Moorcroft's antennae with retailers, and manufacturers ignore constructive retailer comments at their peril.

The last day of 1993 witnessed the demise of Buttercup, Seasons, Wine Magnolia, Lattice, Sunflower and Tudor Rose. In addition, sales of Peter the Pig, Dinosaur, HMS Sirius and Temptation Bowls were concluded. Edwards had been glad to see a final piece of each of them pass into the Museum collection. Once a design has been discontinued, it takes its place in the secondary or 'antique' market. Generally, but not invariably, Moorcroft pottery tends to rise in value some time after discontinuation as collectors move in and scour potential outlets for pieces to complete their individual collections.

Ironically, the lower the volume of sales during the period the range or piece is in production, the higher the value tends to rise in the secondary market, particularly in the short term. Generally speaking, Edwards felt that Moorcroft should never be purchased because of its 'investment value', but only because of the specific aesthetic appeal of an individual piece at the moment of purchase. However, even Edwards admitted the added financial interest of finding perhaps the first or the last piece of a limited edition.

In the life of an art pottery it is always healthy to see design move on, and during the early summer of 1994 Rachel made it clear that she wanted to extend the Butterfly range. John Moorcroft, who had taken Foxglove under his personal wing since the moment of its launch, had started to agitate for an extension of this range, despite production problems as a result of chemical incompatibility in the background colours. Indeed, quite independently, Foxglove had received a substantial boost in profile from an exhibition in Tokyo held in January 1994 at the massive 'Tokyo Dome'. Together with Wedgwood and Minton, Moorcroft had been selected to represent Great Britain at this prestigious trade show.

Moorcroft's Japanese Agent, Yoshi Hibino, had been astute enough to ensure that Japan was the first nation in the world to see Foxglove, and as a result the design received a boost from an unexpected source. The exhibition, opened by their Imperial Highnesses the Prince and Princess Takamado, enabled more than two hundred thousand people to look at the display on the Moorcroft stand. Prince Takamado was particularly enthusiastic about Moorcroft pottery and spent some time extolling its virtues to the assembled entourage. This interest was quickly picked up by Japan's Channel 4 Television, where Foxglove, so lovingly handled by His Imperial Highness, rapidly became a familiar Moorcroft design to the Japanese people. English collectors had formed similar opinions themselves, and once residual problems of colour compatibility had been resolved, an enlarged range of Foxglove was high on the Moorcroft agenda.

Inevitably in the life of art pottery, there is something which breaks the routine or which rears up as a problem requiring a solution. Ken and Hillie Manley had been long-standing members of the Moorcroft Collectors' Club, and both were regular visitors to Open Weekend. Between them they succeeded in breaking Moorcroft's routine. Some time earlier, Ken and Hillie had purchased a racehorse which was given the apt name of 'Moorcroft Boy'. John Moorcroft had been forced to withstand a certain amount of teasing, scowling darkly whenever Hugh suggested he should dress up in jockey's livery and pose with the horse, for the Collectors' Club Newsletter. A series of successes in National Hunt outings over the jumps suggested that Moorcroft Boy was no ordinary horse, and it was Edwards who learned it had been entered for the 1994 Grand National.

Heartsease: 1994 Special Occasions vase. Height 5"

Edwards placed his bet each way with ante-post odds of 40-1 and sat back to watch the race. Right up to and over the last jump, Moorcroft Boy was at or near the front. Two hundred yards from home, he stopped running and virtually walked over the line dropping back from first place to third place in the process. A 'third' was not as good as a first, but it was better than nothing. Edwards was delighted that Moorcroft Pottery had already presented its personal trophy to Ken and Hillie, and at Open Weekend collectors showed their appreciation with one of the loudest rounds of applause Edwards had heard for some time. Shortly after the race, Moorcroft Boy crushed a bone in his neck. Ken and Hillie did not put the horse down; veterinary surgeons performed miracles and two years later, against all the odds, Moorcroft Boy won the Scottish Grand National.

A problem rearing its head in the same year which called for a solution concerned copyright in Moorcroft design. To a company such as Moorcroft copyright is one of its most important assets, and the higher the quality of the product design, the higher the value of the asset. Uncontrolled and unauthorised photography of Moorcroft Pottery and the faking of its art had increased in frequency as the company's reputation grew. The Moorcroft Board would not have known it at the time they made their decisions on copyright, but at the 1996 Spring Fair at Birmingham, a fake Mamoura vase made in China was openly on show on another stand.

The means of putting a stop to such nonsense once and for all was as simple as any legal remedy could be. On each pot, on each lamp produced by Moorcroft there would appear on the base the familiar © symbol with a date added. That date would indicate the date of creation of the original design, and taken together with the copyright symbol would make it impossible for the piece to be illicitly made or used for any photographic purpose other than the private domestic use of the owner of the plate, vase, clock or lamp. Edwards had looked hard at the first pieces bearing the new marks with some satisfaction. Unauthorised production or publication would be followed by an injunction and a Court

Moorcroft Boy

Order for delivery or destruction on oath. The quality of the Moorcroft image was safe, but it gave collectors another 'mark' to contend with.

As a matter of principle, the Moorcroft Board had approved the reintroduction of a loving cup some months earlier, and the shape had been tentatively earmarked for the 1994 Collectors' Club. Quite suddenly and after what seemed like only minimum discussion, Snowdrop appeared as a design on the loving cup. Modern and fresh in the Rachel Bishop idiom, the soft white flower clung to the old loving cup shape in a way that pleased everyone except the Moorcroft photographer whose lens consistently picked out the subtle variations in the shades of dark green which provided the ground colour on the piece. The same dark green monochrome ground created grave difficulties for Works Manager, Justin Emery, whose team had to make it. With production in full swing, good snowdrop loving cups were coming off the kiln trucks at only a tenth of the pace that they should have done. All in all, the 1994 Collectors' Club piece was destined to be slow in production

'Snowdrop' loving cup: Height 6″

terms, and collectors who had already ordered and paid for a piece would justifiably complain. Gill Moorcroft braced herself for a long, hard summer.

Special 'trial' offerings to sell at the 1994 Open Days, the Collectors' Club Secretary had remarked, looked more like 'bin-ends' than collectable pieces. A few pre-1993 trials were still available, but of Rachel's work there was precious little on offer. Even so, Gill somehow found enough to fill a small table of 'Specials'. Rachel, for her part, had designed a pot dubbed Adonis or Pheasant's Eye for the occasion. It was a cheerful piece on an ivory ground with three differently coloured flowers, and the vase on an 80/6″ shape would have sold exceptionally well if only sufficient numbers had been produced. For his part Justin Emery always tended to underestimate collectors' enthusiasm, and for their part, collectors tended to underestimate the problems faced by a hard-pressed Works Manager. The net result was a number of cross collectors who had been unable to buy, and a sharp and immediate increase in the value of Adonis pieces in the secondary market only weeks after Open Weekend. A coaster (not designed as a serious piece, Rachel had emphasised) with a bee at its centre was used as the collectors' piece on which their personal message could be written. An occasional light-hearted design had always been part of the Moorcroft philosophy.

With a little help from television personality, Eric Knowles, it was the Moorcroft decorators who really turned up trumps to make the 1994 Open Days memorable. The moment Eric Knowles, ceramics expert and auctioneer, accepted the Moorcroft invitation to attend the 1994 Open Weekend as guest speaker, success was assured. Eric the Unpredictable would always be matched by Eric the Ceramics Academic, Eric the Connoisseur and Eric the Raconteur.

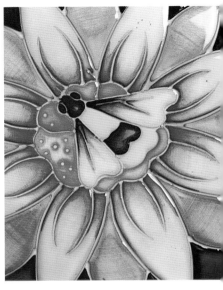

'Bee' coaster – detail

In the event, delighted collectors were also able to enjoy Eric the Auctioneer after Stoke-on-Trent's own auctioneer, Peter Blood, had made way for him to take a few lots at the end of the collectors' auction.

Inevitably this resulted in some hilarious bidding. Until that moment, Peter had kept his audience on the edge of their chairs with moments of great amusement matched by moments of high drama provoked by the Moorcroft decorators' own pieces. Geisha, designed by tube-liner Gill Powell, was a star turn. Hayley Mitchell's Geisha sold for £500 and £590 on the two days of Open Weekend, whilst Marjorie Hill's Geishas were knocked down for £410 and £530 respectively. Catalonia, designed and decorated by Beverley Wilkes with tube-lining by Gill Leese, sold for £610 on Saturday and £580 on Sunday. Coming only a year after her interesting Brittany Vase, Beverley Wilkes and those supporting her had every reason to be pleased. One of the finest Moorcroft paintresses of all time, Wendy Mason, turned her artist's hand and eye to Hunted Hart, designed by Julie Dolan and tube-lined by Marie

Adonis ('Pheasants Eye'): Height 6"

Penkethman. Inevitably collectors showed their approval by clapping vigorously when Peter Blood banged down the hammer at what seemed to four surprised Moorcroft directors a very high price.

Eric the Ceramics Academic and Eric the Raconteur had also been witty and entertaining earlier in the day at the Stoke-on-Trent Museum and Art Gallery. The chosen subject for his lecture, accompanied by slides, was 'Commemorative Wares'. The presentation spanned almost 300 years, and in the last hundred years of selected pieces Moorcroft featured strongly. Special, too, for Open Weekend were sets of limited edition prints of Rachel Bishop's designs for Foxglove and Oberon. It had been Gill Moorcroft's idea to use Rachel's design drawings for prints. A limited edition print, particularly a print of the John Rainford Charger, would be an item of interest for collectors, and in the event a number of contented collectors went home with prints tucked under their arms. In the longer term, Edwards' private view was that those prints would turn out to be a good investment for their owners. Much more importantly, in the short term they were something different and something pleasant to hang on the wall and enjoy.

'Hunted Hart' by Wendy Mason. 'Geisha' by Marjorie Hill: Height 12"

TWELVE

England and Abroad

The discontinuation of Sally Dennis sunflower design was not the reason for Rachel's drive to introduce a sunflower design of her own. As a designer Rachel had not looked closely at the falling sales figures, preferring instead to rely on her own observations of sunflowers and the images they provoked in her mind. She had listened to the word 'cool' which Hugh had often used to describe Hypericum, and inevitably the word 'warm' insinuated itself into her thoughts. You do not have to be a scholar to realise that 'warm' is the opposite of 'cool', and thoughts of the word 'warm' translated into sunflowers – Rachel's own sunflowers standing majestically in the fields of southern France during high summer.

Additionally she had begun to be cautious in her responses to the words 'traditional Moorcroft', often used to describe anything which had a vaguely blue ground. In point of fact, Sally's Sunflowers had faded in popularity largely because of the limited extent of the range and the size of the pieces. From her own observations as a designer, the blue ground which Sally had used to provide a backcloth for her sunflowers caused Rachel difficulty, mixing as it did, images of coolness and warmth together. To Rachel the two colours were aesthetically incompatible in the context of sunflowers, and as she concentrated on this fact, there flashed into her mind a 'warm' sunflower theme in the Bishop idiom, unencumbered by a blue ground.

It was Gill Moorcroft who first announced to Hugh that something interesting was in the wings. Gill always used the word 'interesting' when she was unsure about whether to be associated with the project or not. With a minimum of artistic fuss, Rachel's new

FACING: *Inca, tallest vase 12″* RIGHT: *Inca, rear vase 10″. Discontinued 1996*

*13" Kyoto vase. facing: Kyoto vase detail.
Discontinued 1996*

Sunflower range was brought forward, trialled and assembled. Abandoning her conventional position of neutrality, Gill announced that the design was 'different'. This meant that as far as she was concerned production could go ahead, but without her formal blessing. Embracing twelve pots and a plate as well as four lamps, the design was dubbed Inca – a name offered by Gill in the absence of anything better from her fellow directors.

While Butterfly and Foxglove were lining themselves up for extensions to their ranges and Inca trials were running their final course, Moorcroft collectors themselves had responded with unexpected vigour to the Newsletter invitation issued in May 1994 to write to Rachel Bishop and request a small range of Kyoto pieces. The exhibition vase had sold out within sixteen weeks of its launch, suggesting that there were a large number of disappointed collectors about. In the event, the response from collectors was so strong that by the end of July five pieces to make up a representative Kyoto range on a different blue ground had already been designed, and by mid September prototypes had been approved for production in 1995 with little or no fuss.

There was a touch of mischief in Rachel's choice of ground colour for her Kyoto pieces. By any definition it was a 'traditional' Moorcroft blue. The design, however, was anything but traditional, and no one could seriously assert that it was. If the design failed, then it would be a failure of a range using traditional Moorcroft blue. Success or failure in Rachel's book of rules had nothing to do with 'tradition'. Tradition was dangerous in art, and its disciples ran serious risk of failure. Success or failure depended on the quality of design, a balanced use of subtle colour and the hard work put in by Moorcroft's quality retailers at home and abroad. It had next to nothing to do with tradition.

Edwards had been noncommittal about the introduction of the Inca range, rather more on the ground that a sunflower design could never be used on small

*Kyoto group. Diameter of charger 14"
Discontinued 1996*

pieces simply by reason of the size of the flower itself. As a result, the 1995 catalogue offerings comprised two new ranges, Inca and Kyoto, neither of which contained pieces which could really be defined as 'small'. For Edwards, a balanced presentation which included small pieces was good for collectors. That said, he kept his thoughts to himself and Inca was put into production with Kyoto.

The early months of 1994 had been an exhausting experience for both the Moorcrofts and the Edwards. After trade shows in Birmingham and Frankfurt, John had once again toured Canada to consolidate Moorcroft's new direct marketing initiative. Then, with virtually no break, he had been joined by Maureen, and together they had introduced Moorcroft Pottery to the Arab world at an impressive trade show in Dubai. Both still recount dourly the number of times they were invited to barter on a price for the pieces exhibited on the Moorcroft stand! To relax and give themselves a treat, the Edwards watched the Moorcrofts travel to Antigua to sell Moorcroft Pottery in the West Indies, and the Moorcrofts watched the Edwards fly to Tahiti to introduce the pottery to the Polynesian Islands of the South Pacific.

Both couples returned determined to find some use for Frangipani – that loveliest of all flowers with its simple contours, its fragrance and its subtlety of colour. The only difference was that synonymous with Frangipani in Tahiti were the famous black pearls and the almost translucent greenish black oysters in which the black pearls grow. At the close of the Autumn Fair in September 1994 at Birmingham, Gill acquired from another stand showing exotic plants a fine specimen of the Frangipani tree for Rachel to draw from. Between them, the Moorcroft Board had dropped the heaviest possible hint about a Frangipani design, though Rachel herself had remained silent. However enthusiastic the Edwards and the Moorcrofts might be, Frangipani was not on Rachel's design agenda.

Art pottery is all about dreams which in turn become ideas, which then translate into an experience and from experience into reality. Most people experience memorable sensations – the fragrance of a lovely flower, the flight of a dragonfly through the reeds on the edge of a pond on a summer's afternoon or a daffodil

FACING: *Lamia Limited Edition vase: Height 20"*

Daffodil: Height 14"

speckled with frost on an early spring morning – but not all can respond or have both the strength of will and skill of a good designer to encapsulate that experience into an art form. Rachel had watched dragonflies skim over the surface of a pond in her mother's garden on the edge of the New Forest, and that simple event had triggered a series of processes in her mind which in an artist are called 'inspiration'. Inspired, she began to move down her own design road to reality.

Back at the Works, Rachel's continuing need for 'green fixes' had already become part of Moorcroft folklore, and it was not surprising to those who knew her well that the New Forest pond and its dragonflies would translate into ceramic art. Lamia (as it was later called) was the design Rachel introduced to the Moorcroft Board as a first sketch in April 1994. Green was a colour considered essential in a Moorcroft catalogue presentation. If Rainforest, Finches Teal and perhaps Mamoura were to go out of production, then a fresh green theme was called for. Rachel was in her element, and by August a large new prestige vase for display at the International Spring Fair at Birmingham in 1995 was ready for approval.

The finished piece was quite the loveliest vase Maureen, Gill and Hugh had ever seen in their lives. It breathed the spirit of Lamia, the water nymph in Keats' classic poem of the same name. Each element of the design flowed across the vase from one part to another with the result that the whole design appeared to wrap itself around the piece, as if each had belonged to the other forever. John was in Australia when the piece first emerged from the kiln, but the remainder of the Board, not least of all Gill, were stunned into silence. In the world of art pottery, success is not something which is achieved the whole of the time. If it is achieved just a little of the time, the potter is doing well. To achieve something little short of pure magic is a rare experience in a single lifetime. It also brings an unusual problem in its wake. A piece where the word 'magic' is appropriate tends to set standards for the designer which are appreciably higher thereafter.

Maureen had no wish to see John Moorcroft's catalogue printing timetable delayed, and because John was in Australia design consultation had to be dealt with on the telephone, no easy task. The Board knew that a new limited edition vase was necessary to replace the Rose and Bud vase and box, but it was something of a relief to find that sufficient Trellis clocks remained to enable the edition to be offered to the public for a second time in 1995. At least that had been the position in July 1994 when Hugh had first investigated the sales of the Trellis clocks. But ceramics are all about the unexpected, and by September orders in hand for Trellis clocks made it quite clear that the edition of 250 would be sold out by Christmas or even earlier. As a result, two new limited editions were necessary and not one as everybody had hoped earlier in the summer.

A Daffodil design had been offered by Rachel as replacement for the Rose and Bud pieces. The chosen shape had been modelled from a 14″ Florian ware vase during August by Trevor Critchlow, and initially the new shape had been identified for use in the extended Foxglove range. Its height alone made the piece significant in its own right. Initially, Rachel had introduced her design to the Board on both a

celadon and an ivory body. Edwards had instantly disliked the autumnal daffodils which resulted from the use of the celadon body. Spring flowers, he had complained, were bright and fresh. Daffodils were no exception. However, he was overruled by the Moorcrofts and his wife, and the celadon body went forward to further trialling.

The design itself was, however, generally liked, and the use of leaf panels to frame each flower had been a design technique successfully applied by William Moorcroft in his early work at the turn of the century. A rash of celadon pieces appeared – six in all, Edwards pointed out sourly, plus a new colouring of the design on an ivory ground. It was, Rachel had announced, not sensible to abandon the ivory body concept altogether. Hugh said nothing since the others probably assumed he had been outmanoeuvring the Board, which was not in fact true. He had said nothing to Rachel, and neither had he been consulted by her. Ultimately, with the designer's support, the ivory ground daffodil won

England: Height 9″

the day at the next design meeting, and after a number of subtle colour changes had been incorporated the vase was approved for production in an edition limited to two hundred and fifty pieces.

By the time it had become clear beyond all doubt that the Trellis clock edition would sell out before 1995, John and Gill had left for a holiday in Kenya. In their absence, and to provide collectors with a substitute, the Edwards pressed on with a Rachel Bishop design on a new and finely finished torchère shape, which Hugh dubbed England as soon as he saw the first prototype. He was not particularly fond of the piece, but it was adequate. After one or two colour changes, a second trial of the England vase emerged from the kiln on the day the Moorcrofts returned from their autumn holiday. Gill did not like either piece, and said so. John was indifferent, rather as Hugh had been, but after a day's exposure to his wife, John decided that he, too, did not like the piece, and the two of them initiated some slight changes to the structure of the flowers.

In the meantime, Hugh had left for a lecture tour of the United States and Japan on legal and financial matters for Richards Butler, and a phone call from Maureen to her husband in Chicago alerted him to the possible change of heart on John's part. Edwards' financial instincts joined forces with his collector's instincts, and together they left him in no doubt that a second new limited edition piece was crucial to balance Moorcroft's 1995 presentation. Accordingly, he faxed the Works from Chicago saying that either the catalogue printing was to be held up until a new design was trialled and approved by all those concerned, or England went through for production. The choice lay with the Moorcrofts. Two weeks later, an England vase incorporating the Moorcrofts' amendments was being photographed for the catalogue.

THIRTEEN

Pushing out the Boat

At a design meeting held in June 1994, a tentative sketch of the centenary design and production timetable had been drawn up. Edwards knew that all design work for centenary pieces would have to be completed no later than June 1996. This would enable photography for published material to be completed; it would enable the company to plan out its events for 1997, and it would enable Justin Emery to ensure that Moorcroft had the correct level of staff to meet the demands a centenary year would entail.

The key feature of the centenary presentation was to be a set of special pieces by Rachel Bishop. Additionally, John and Hugh also persuaded Walter, who would turn 80 in 1997, to create a design of his own choosing on a shape of his own choice. Walter had responded positively to the idea, telling them both that he had a point to make and intended to make it. Even so, Edwards was convinced that something more was needed to celebrate the occasion. Provided the necessary expertise could be dredged up from a hundred years of experience in making Moorcroft pottery, the greatest challenge of all would be to make a centenary pot designed by William Moorcroft, the founding father of the company.

To reproduce a design in somebody's collection might be construed as harmful and was to be avoided. The Board agreed that much without hesitation. It was also at Edwards' suggestion that the Board looked once more at the Florian yacht design on the old glass photographic plates, with a view to confirming their earlier decision to experiment with the past. Notwithstanding strong reservations from Gill, articulated on the ground that it might upset the antiques-dealing community, it was unanimously decided to take the project forward. An attempt would be made to recreate the old Florian yacht vase, making it clear on the face of the vase itself that it had been made in 1997. Additionally, only contemporary marks would appear on the base.

Photographer Michael Bruce was consulted once more. Before returning the old glass photographic plates to the Moorcroft family, Michael had taken negatives from which he had produced a large set of prints in different sizes. From these prints he discovered that not only was it possible to calculate the size of the original piece, but also details of the design. Michael Bruce had first pointed out that people could be seen on the yachts featured on the original vase, and he calculated with the aid of his photographic prints that the original vase had been 9″ high. This he had been done by measuring the width of the original tube-lining on a James Macintyre & Co vase of similar vintage, and then applying the measurement to the various 'blow-ups' he had prepared. The measurement fitted only the 9″ piece, and Edwards had been convinced.

Justin Emery was apprehensive as soon as he was approached. Justin's schooling and family history had been steeped in ceramic colours. Colours were known to be Justin's strong point, but to be asked to recreate a piece of pottery which had first been made by William Moorcroft almost a hundred years earlier was a task quite unlike any other. Because the size and shape of the vase were both known, Trevor Critchlow, the Moorcroft mould-maker, was put to work to model, block and case the shape of the old vase after profiling it from the original photograph.

Even so, to rediscover colour pigments not used for decades, was a daunting task. More significantly, the glazes on old Macintyre pottery had contained lead, something wholly unacceptable at Moorcroft today. To concentrate on the project, Edwards had deduced, would take Justin's mind off the long-term production difficulties the centenary year would entail. Of even greater significance was the fact that sooner or later, and certainly before his own colour research could translate itself into the final trial, Justin would be obliged to seek Rachel's help to put the original William Moorcroft design onto his new pot. Put another way, the Works Manager would be obliged to work on the project in tandem with the designer in a way and with an intensity never required of them before.

The Moorcrofts were still on holiday in Kenya when Justin opened the drawer of his desk to show Edwards his first experimental pieces. To Edwards, they looked remarkably like a pair of 'blue on blue' Florian foxglove vases. One, Justin announced, had been made on a pure

Early photograph of the Florian yacht vase

FACING: The 1997 version of William Moorcroft's Florian yacht vase
INSET: Marie Penkethman tube-lining the Florian yacht vase

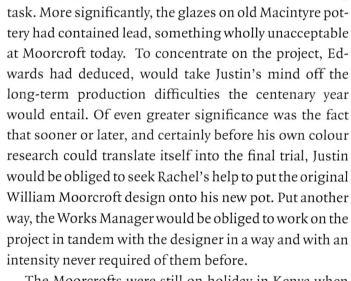

white body and the other on Moorcroft's traditional ivory body. At first glance, both looked uncannily reminiscent of their ancestors, but since William Moorcroft had never produced a Foxglove design, it did not matter. It had been, Justin remarked casually, a difficult exercise, but his startling discovery had been confirmation of the fact that the old Florian vases produced at James Macintyre & Co had without doubt been made with ivory bodies, rather than the pure white bodies which might have been expected from a manufacturer of industrial porcelain as some commentators had suggested.

At the end of August, on their way home from a trip to drought-stricken North Wales, the Edwards had called in at the Works. Moorcroft had, of course, shut down for the late summer Wakes Holiday, but it was a good time to talk about the ship vase project. The Edwards were joined by Justin Emery for dinner at the Potters Club in Stoke-on-Trent. The Works Manager was in good form, but the smiles faded when Hugh mentioned the Ship vase. A hundred years ago, minus perhaps eighteen months or thereabouts, the old 'blue on blue' Florian vases made by William Moorcroft and his staff at James Macintyre and Co had been decorated by first dipping the unfired clay body of the piece into an 'engobe' of blue coloured slip (liquid clay). To put an engobe of coloured slip on a raw clay pot had the effect of putting a thin blue skin over the original uncoloured body. At the same time it provided a uniform ground colour for the decorators.

Not only had Justin found it extremely difficult to make an exact match of colour for the base 'engobe', but the old firing temperatures in the coal-fired bottle kilns used at the time were, to say the least, uncertain. An incorrect firing temperature would either adversely affect the colour of the engobe, or, even worse, cause the engobe to peel off the piece to which it had been applied. Hugh reminded Justin that many old Moorcroft pieces had been created by using coloured engobes, including the famous Cornflower and Spanish Patterns.

Justin's reply went to the heart of the problem. William Moorcroft was in the business of creating colour, not recreating it. Accordingly, any result achieved by William could be labelled as correct, and that was an option not open to Justin. It was as simple as that. Hugh and

Justin Emery, Works Manager and alchemist

Maureen were determined to press on and solve the problems. By the end of the evening so, too, was Justin.

The first batch of colour trials using a blue engobe had not been successful. Although Justin had already confirmed his earlier finding that William Moorcroft's Art Pottery department at James Macintyre & Co generally used ivory clay bodies, his own trials had an underlying green tinge which Justin had found disturbing and which Rachel said was off the mark. Like all good artists, she had been right in her colour diagnosis as had Justin, the colour expert. In strict theory, the blue selected by Justin should have worked. He had already consulted widely with a number of colour suppliers to the ceramics industry, and diligent to the end he kept on trying. A fresh blue was selected and trialled but the result still remained the same. The irritating undertone of green was still there. Justin, the man of colour, acknowledged defeat.

A month later, during an animated conversation with a friend, he had been reminded that blue and yellow mixed together made green. The truth exploded in Justin's mind. Ivory clay as opposed to pure white clay had a faintly 'cream' tint, often used to great effect by William Moorcroft and more recently by Rachel with her Butterfly range. Cream as a colour is achieved by mixing yellow with white. Eliminating the yellow, retaining the white, and using a pure white clay slip mixed with blue for the engobe should solve the problem. The final batch of trials were an almost perfect match to the Museum vase which Justin had been using as his marker. Gill looked at the new colour trials as they came out of the glost kiln and snapped at Hugh crossly. To recreate the Florian 'blue on blue' effect could seriously reduce the value of her personal collection of old Moorcroft; dealers should not know that Moorcroft still had the skills to make pottery in the old idiom.

Edwards disagreed. Jobs were more important than trophy pots, and hardship for the dealing fraternity was unlikely. As a breed they were born survivors with an

Test pieces in various blues (top)
Foxglove blue trials (below)

ability to scavenge any pickings of whatever vintage had value. It should be a matter of pride, Edwards confided to his wife later, that Moorcroft was still able to make the pots that its ancestors made and much more in addition. In that way skills improved and reached out to wider horizons. If crooks copied Moorcroft and forged pieces to deceive innocent people, it was a matter for the laws of England to control. In any event, he had concluded, if value depended on the inability of the original maker to recreate, then the value was false. Value should depend upon intrinsic quality of the piece, and age could occasionally add its own dimension.

Within weeks the first prototype of the old Florian Yacht vase was ready for inspection. One ship's flag carried the date 1897 and the other 1997. On the base appeared the centenary mark 'H' while the copyright mark was the equally uncompromising © 1996. William Moorcroft's contribution to the pottery which proudly carries his name was ready for an enthusiastic public.

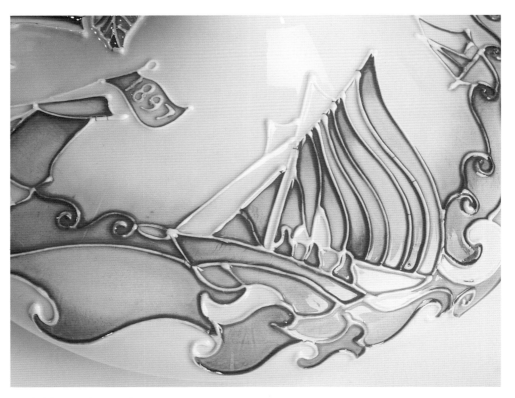

Detail of the 1997 Florian yacht vase

FOURTEEN

The President and the Cockatoo

The British Ceramic Manufacturers' Federation is a body which monitors the ceramics industry nationwide year in and year out, acting as its official voice when required. Although a relatively small company, W. Moorcroft Plc had been a member of the BCMF for a number of years and John Moorcroft was the company's nominated representative. In June 1993 John had been asked if he would like to become Vice President of the Federation from July 1993-1994 and President for the ensuing year, 1994-1995. Hugh and Maureen were told of the news shortly thereafter.

Whether anticipating some kind of veto at the announcement, Edwards' large smile came as a relief to John who pressed his advantage. Edwards had to appreciate, John pointed out, that from the summer of 1994 to the summer of 1995 presidential duties would make considerable inroads into his time at Moorcroft. It was an honour for the company, there was no doubt of that, and Edwards was quick to say so. Until that moment only the large companies had featured in the Federation's politics, and for Moorcroft to be asked to provide the President was a sure sign that the earth itself was moving in Stoke-on-Trent. Maureen gave Gill a big hug, while Hugh contented himself by remarking that the Federation did not know what they were letting themselves in for!

Later that year, after the first announcement of his appointment as Vice President, John asked Hugh to help him find a guest speaker for the BCMF's annual dinner. He knew that Edwards had contacts among the great and the good in London. Among them would be all manner of possible candidates for guest speaker at John's presidential dinner.

Top of John's list of Hugh's friends was the Right Honourable John Smith MP, QC, leader of Her Majesty's loyal opposition. Hugh had looked at his old friend with mild surprise at the request, but had asked the leader of the Labour Party notwithstanding. His acceptance produced as much joy in the Moorcroft camp as it produced great sorrow three months later, when John Smith tragically died of a heart attack. Once again Edwards scanned his list of contacts, pondering on the possibility that the new-found confidence in the emerging post-recession export markets was probably a key issue for the Federation. What was needed was a good economist, a financial expert, someone who would seek to understand the Federation's problems during John's year as President.

In the end, it was Rupert Pennant-Rea whom Edwards eventually contacted. The Deputy Governor of the Bank of England was an able speaker and would amuse and entertain John's guests at the Federation's dinner tables, as well as provide serious comments about the ceramics industry. Although Hugh was pleased when the Deputy Governor accepted the Moorcroft invitation, fate intervened and dealt another blow. Six weeks before the scheduled date of the BCMF dinner, a scandal broke around the Deputy Governor as a result of his friendship with a financial journalist, and he resigned his position. Apologies were tendered to John, and the search for yet another replacement speaker became a matter of urgency.

This time Edwards turned again to his friends in the Labour Party, and the political tree was shaken. One of Labour's senior Euro-MP's, John Tomlinson, cancelled another engagement in Birmingham to attend, and the crisis passed. Edwards had told the guest speaker privately that he was worried both about his health and his morals, but on the day, after quips about both, Tomlinson broke new ground and spoke about the ceramics industry in the context of Europe – an innovation which John Moorcroft had been pleased to initiate. The occasion also marked the retirement of Alf Clowes, leader of the Ceramic and Allied Trade Union and a greatly respected figure in the ceramics industry. After a Clowes speech which commanded a standing ovation, John Moorcroft presented both Alf and John Tomlinson with a large Foxglove vase to mark an extremely happy and prestigious occasion.

From July 1994 to July 1995, it had become a matter of concern to the Edwards that John's presidential duties might prove to be altogether too much for him. The last thing that Edwards wanted was a Moorcroft heart attack. John had laughingly brushed the suggestion aside, but when in the late summer he had a dizzy turn he did not fight Edwards' suggestion to have a thorough medical check-up. Not that Edwards himself was in any position to talk. In March 1994, after his role in restoring the profitability of the firm's Property Group following the property slump of 1990-3, Hugh's Partners at Richards Butler had put him in charge of the firm's

FACING: *Cockatoo vase and plate: Vase 10"*

Corporate and Commercial Group with general brief to rejuvenate its structure, redefine its objectives and steer it in a direction which would take full advantage of economic recovery.

That assignment on its own was yet another challenge – or cause of stress, as his wife had darkly muttered. During their time in Tahiti, husband and wife had discussed together the possibility of Edwards becoming Managing Partner at Richards Butler, a proposition which had rumbled around for some weeks. In the event, both had concluded that Edwards as a full-time administrator in a law firm was not on. There were others who were better equipped to undertake the role and that message was relayed to Hugh's colleagues on the Richards Butler Board immediately after the Edwards returned from the South Pacific. Hugh stayed on as head of the Corporate and Commercial Group, to help it recover its position at Richards Butler as the engine house of the firm. His task was to steer the Group in a direction that, in simple terms, spelt continued international expansion and greater profitability.

To fulfill his obligations to his Partners at Richards Butler, the remainder of 1994 brought a punishing schedule of travel for Edwards, including a three week round-the-world trip which saw him lecturing at the International Development and Research Council World Congress in Dallas, Texas. From there he travelled to Tokyo for a seminar on cross-border loans at the headquarters of the Japanese equivalent to the Confederation of British Industry. The name of the game, his Partners at Richards Butler had reminded him, was continued promotion of the firm's existing international profile. Edwards found this amusing, recalling that John himself must have travelled many thousands of miles during the preceding four years to act as ambassador for Moorcroft.

In late summer 1994, John had set out for Australia with a prototype 10″ plate showing a white cockatoo specially requested by Moorcroft's Australian distributor, Philip Allen. Both the large and the small Blue Gum vases had been resounding successes, and the idea was to follow up with further pieces designed solely for the Australian market. The Moorcroft Board had not particularly liked the idea of pots carrying a cockatoo design, but Philip Allen had insisted that a bird should be featured and the design process had moved forward accordingly. The initial trials showed a pure white bird with a yellow crest against a backcloth of blue-green leaves, red tube-lined flowers and a really bright blue sky.

Philip Allen was not keen on the sky, which seemed more appropriate to a Caribbean setting than for Australia. Australian skies were bright and clear and

Rachel's sky was revised accordingly. Even so, its monochrome ground spelt potential trouble for the Moorcroft painters, and that fact alone carried with it the high risk of an unacceptable level of 'seconds'. In the opinion of the Moorcroft Board, monochrome grounds had begun to feature too much in some of the more recent Rachel Bishop designs, and this message was passed through to her in a number of subtle ways. The revival of the softer, 'washed' grounds had been something which the former design team had fought long and hard to bring about, and the last thing that either the Edwards or the Moorcrofts wanted at this moment was to start reinventing the monochrome wheel.

Perhaps more significantly, John had started to react against design influences coming from a distributor or retailer rather than the Moorcroft designer. As a result, Edwards had found it easy to support John's point of view on the ground colour of the Cockatoo vase and plate when Philip Allen visited his London office during the autumn. As it turned out, however, Edwards liked Philip Allen. He was a businessman with a reliable feel for quality and value. Bad businessmen and businesswomen who are failures in one way or another will always blame their suppliers should things go wrong with their business. Philip Allen had always been supportive of Moorcroft through feast and famine and he was a good friend. More importantly he did an excellent job promoting Moorcroft's collectability in Australia and had introduced Moorcroft to many of Australia's prestigious retail outlets.

At the end of the London meeting, it was agreed there would be two cockatoo pieces. The first would be a 10″ plate produced in an edition of 350 pieces, and the second a large vase. The 4/10″ shape was agreed for the vase, and the vase edition limited to 60. The price for the pieces would be settled as soon as all production difficulties had been identified and ironed out. It was those same production problems that would drive the delivery schedule, and Edwards made it clear that Philip Allen would not see the first pieces of either the plate or the vase before late autumn of 1995 at the earliest.

FIFTEEN

Guns And Cherries

Propped on one elbow, Edwards surveyed the Sea of Marmaris reflectively and the small sailing boats plying their way in both directions, coming it seemed from nowhere, but going no doubt somewhere, their small triangular flags flapping ineffectively in the warm breeze. For a passing second they might just have been the Florian yachts captured on film by the Victorian photographer a hundred years earlier. The Turkish sunshine was hot, and a huge pine tree on the mountain side provided welcome shade as well as a soft, sweet-smelling bed of pine needles to lie on. Nothing could have been more peaceful. Edwards moved and eased his body to the ground, looking up at a bright blue sky which acted as a backdrop to the branches, pine needles and cones above. Philip Allen might just have been right about the original blue ground of the Cockatoo vase. Perhaps it had been just a bit too blue. Rachel had been irritated by his apparent change of heart about the colour at the time, but life goes on. It was neither the design nor the issue on which to stand and fight.

Rachel had certainly been right about the pine needles and cones on the 1995 Year Plate. Those above Edwards' head reminded him of the piece, although Turkey had no red squirrels to leap and dart among the branches of the pine trees that grew in profusion in the countryside. The holiday was a welcome break from what had been an excruciatingly tiring March and April. Not only had April seen out the Richards Butler financial year end, but also completion of Moorcroft's third and exceptionally hectic accounting quarter. For the man of commerce both had been par for the course, but Edwards guessed that the combination was beginning to take its toll.

Additionally, in early March his Partners at Richards Butler had dispatched him to the former Soviet Republic of Azerbaijan on the edge of the Caspian Sea to sign up a contract for the supply of legal services for a national privatisation project of key manufacturing industries. Coming in to land at Baku airport in atrocious

FACING: 1995 8" *Squirrel plate*, 5" *Summer Lawn*, *and Morello bowl: Length* 9"

weather, the pilot appeared to miscalculate his approach to the runway, and the great aircraft had almost ditched in a nearby swamp. Never in his life had Edwards been more pleased to hear the roar of the engines as the plane surged back into the grey clouds leaving behind a trail of spray. W. Moorcroft Plc, as well as Richards Butler and his family, had almost been deprived of one of their key members. Only later had he established that the radar had been switched off as the result of a 'few local problems'.

Those local problems turned out to have been an attempted coup, and for the third time in his life Edwards found himself in the centre of civil unrest. That he was staying in a Presidential apartment in Baku and scheduled to meet the Deputy Prime Minister the following day did nothing to increase his confidence, and to those who subsequently took the trouble to ask, his reply, usually accompanied by a wry smile, was that he was a professional coward! Edwards had already witnessed the violent arrival of Colonel Gadafy in Libya, as well as the more controlled arrival of the Ayatollah Khomeni in Iran. Experience derived from both events had taught him that the further away a person was from the epicentre of political and military turmoil, the greater the safety factor tended to be.

A hard Russian bed in his apartment and the sound of sporadic gun and mortar fire are not conducive to sleep. Edwards remained fully clothed and tried hard to shut out the nastier side of life outside with more pleasant thoughts of the Works. In the morning, Gill would be muttering about her new computer; Justin would be trying to maintain good order and discipline in a work place where art made the very concept doubtful; John would be fretting about his Canadian trip and the lack of television interest which Canada, unlike Australia, showed in his visits. Beverley Potts in the office would still be fuming at an article by Sean Slattery in the December Newsletter which had caused all of the Works' telephone lines to be blocked for a week while she tried hard to direct collectors who wanted to buy Rachel's Lamia vases to the most appropriate retailer.

The Turkish holiday had been preceded by a piece of extremely sad news for Hugh and Maureen. Their old friend in the law, John Rainford, had been diagnosed as suffering from advanced lung cancer. Without John, Edwards' career would have taken a totally different course, and Moorcroft's Oberon range would not exist. Life had a strange habit of bringing people and events together and then severing them mercilessly for no apparent good reason. Goodness is a human quality in short supply, and John Rainford had been a good friend and colleague.

In the world of the mid-1990's, where man's only God seemed to be personal performance and where his only object in life appeared to be to making money, it was unusual in the extreme for anyone to regard an English clearing bank as an object of affection rather than fear. National Westminster Bank had been Moorcroft's bankers for more than seventy-five years, and through the bad times as well as the good their umbrella had always been available when it rained. The life of a potter can be a precarious one, with success one day matched by failure the next. Moorcroft had been no exception to the rule and there was no reason why it should have been. Edwards' first contact with the local branch in 1986 had been good and the outcome positive.

Edwards frequently recalls his early meetings with the Bank's local Manager, John Webster: the preparation of his financial plan, cashflow forecasts, and borrowing requirements. In the end without any personal guarantees, the Bank through John Webster had approved the facilities required, and Edwards had assumed financial control of Moorcroft as the *quid pro quo*. Edwards liked John Webster, all six foot and six inches of him. The Bank Manager was an honourable man who kept his word, and Edwards liked people who stayed true to their word. Support was never withdrawn and encouragement was always available. Such people are rare in the world of commercial finance, and quite early on Edwards reached a point in their relationship where he actually enjoyed the prospect of their regular meetings. All good things come to an end, however, and in April 1995, after a series of promotions within the Bank, John Webster retired. Edwards was sad. It was the end of another chapter in the Moorcroft story, and the huge turnout at his retirement party suggested many other bank customers felt the same way.

Admittedly, the bad news was tinged with good news. John's Presidency of the British Ceramic Manufacturer's Federation had been a great credit to W. Moorcroft Plc. To be awarded a Royal Warrant as a result of sales to a member of the Royal family was one thing, but to be elected President of a major manufacturing industry in this country suggests something far more important. The contribution made by your company to that industry will have been judged by those harshest of all critics – your competitors. Edwards was proud of John in the same way that he was proud of the rebirth of the company which had made John's presidency possible. He was proud of all the great skills in the work force which make up the close Moorcroft corporate family, of the hard work and effort put in by the salesmen, and the loyalty, flair and perception of Moorcroft retailers. Moorcroft once again stood among the ranks of the best in the world in terms of ceramic quality and value. Like nostalgia, joy and pride take many forms, and Edwards still recalls with pleasure the moment when Gill Moorcroft whispered in his ear towards the end of the President's Annual Dinner that John would not even have been there without him! The applause from the audience at the end of the President's speech almost drowned the remark as well as Edwards' reply.

Shortly before the Edwards had left for their holiday in Turkey, leading paintress Wendy Mason had married, and so, too, had Rachel Bishop. Both had assured the Moorcroft Board that they would continue to work under their maiden names, although Edwards reconciled himself to the thought that there were two more names to remember: Mrs. Thorne (Wendy) and Mrs. Prescott-Walker (Rachel). Edwards had an appalling memory for names, which was perhaps why he had made little objection when Gill announced that the name for the 1995 Special Occasions vase would be Summer Lawn. In the November 1994 Newsletter, Moorcroft collectors had been asked by Editor Maureen Edwards to suggest names for the 1995 vase. The response had been enthusiastic, and Summer Lawn had emerged as the favourite in Gill's mind.

Market day at Fethiye was as busy and as interesting as any market in the world. The Edwards loved markets, and the fruit, vegetables, eggs and cheese were a joy to look at. Late May in Turkey was the season of the Morello cherry, and some of the market stalls were stacked high with the fruit. The image was not lost on Maureen who drew her husband's attention to the soft red cherries still attached to their green stalks some of which still carried the brown remnants of cherry blossom. The Collectors' Club oval bowl, Morello, seemed to be as pretty as the fruit it represented. Once again, Edwards had to admit to his wife that Gill had been right about the name. That was always the problem. Gill's names were either totally right or totally wrong. The difficulty was establishing which was which.

A further contributing factor to the Edwards' exhaustion at the end of April had been the May Newsletter. Newsletters were time-consuming items to put together in an attractive and readable form for Moorcroft Collectors, who had a good eye for quality. As Editor, Maureen had spent many hours co-ordinating the written copy, assembling photographs and checking factual data. Edwards himself had suggested that the Moorcrofts' collection of mugs should feature on the

Malahide: detail showing retailer's mark

FACING: *Malahide. A 5″ vase made exclusively for retailer James Macintyre & Co, Leeds*

front cover. Maureen had been doubtful about the idea at first, but the final result had proved very successful. It had also been the May Newsletter which had broken the news of the dramatic arrival of Leeds Retailer, James Macintyre & Co Ltd and their lovely shop in the Victoria Quarter. Proprietor Debbie Edwards had commissioned Malahide, a lovely vase on the 152/5″ shape. The design featured the Australian bottlebrush shrub. Subtle use of red tube-lining and the yellow stamenal tips of the flowers made an exceptionally attractive combination, which Rachel had set neatly against light green leaves and a dark blue-green ground. Edwards had privately regretted that the edition had been limited to two hundred pieces, his collector's instincts telling him that the vase was destined to be an interesting investment for its few privileged owners around the world. It was also significant that James Macintyre & Co Ltd was back in business as a name in the world of Moorcroft. If the Edwards' visit to Turkey had coincided with the season of the Morello cherry, it had also coincided with the poppy season. Never before had Edwards seen so many lovely poppies growing in profusion in such a beautiful, natural setting. Some of the fields looked almost blood red. Other fields had been planted with poppies of a cultivated variety which varied in colour from purple to orange, their grey-blue leaves moving gently in the early summer breeze. Hugh knew that Rachel Bishop loved poppies. He had seen some 'angry' poppies in her design studio in Stoke-on-Trent, no doubt borne out of some artistic frustration or another, but he also knew that her original design portfolio included some magnificent specimens. The Moorcroft designer seemed to move most comfortably from a red colour base, and anything in the orange/red/purple/pink stable had a good chance of striking an artistic chord. Perhaps Poppies would feature on her design agenda one day as a result. Privately Hugh hoped so. The Turkish holiday had been a good one, and the Edwards, fully recovered, were ready for the 1995 Open Weekend immediately on their return.

SIXTEEN

Shaping the Future

The fifth and final ginger jar made for B. & W. Thornton featured images taken from Shakespeare's play, 'Cymbeline'. Rachel had succeeded in completing the design work before her April wedding, leaving the task of preparing its flyer with Maureen. The design wove together bluebells, cowslips, violets and primroses in a way that stirred Edwards' collector's instincts, and he had little doubt about its success. 'King Lear' had been Thornton's theme for their ginger jar the preceding year. For the first time in sixty years, ripe corn was used as a design feature. With the corn came Shakespeare's 'furrow weeds' – words taken directly from the play itself. Edwards loved the King Lear design and the rich green and dark blue washed ground Rachel had used to set if off. The design was complete: it wrapped itself round the ginger jar without a break; the colours were a joy to look at, and it had a simplicity which turned it from an average piece of pottery into a great piece of pottery. It was also the only ginger jar in the last three of the series where the designer had been given a totally free hand.

The Moorcroft Board looked hard at the Moorcroft catalogues which had been printed since the departure of the former design team in 1992. Gill had not liked some of the printer's efforts in the 1995 catalogue, any more than she had liked the overtone of pink in the 1994 catalogue. As was Gill's habit, she reminded her husband of the fact to make sure that others would not forget it. The Edwards and the Moorcrofts had spent their 1995 Easter Holiday thinking about shape rather than colour. Shape was of particular interest at that time. As the summer season approached it usually became clear if a range required 'freshening' – another way of saying that some pieces in the range were failing to capture the imagination of Moorcroft customers. Sometimes this was because the range itself had become 'tired', but more often than not it simply meant that one or two shapes were unsuccessful for the design in question and needed to be replaced by new and more sympathetic shapes carrying the same design.

Rachel had successfully supervised the arrival of the 121/14" shape in Foxglove and, on the premise that something more was required, had also persuaded Justin to instruct mould-maker, Trevor Critchlow, to make a refined 'torchère' shape, known at the Works as the 87 shape. The 87 shape ultimately appeared both as a 6" and as a 9" vase, also decorated with Foxglove. In production terms, there had been added benefit in the clay shop as soon as Rachel designed the 1995 Daffodil vase to the 121 shape and the England vase to the 87/9" shape. Her motive had been to ease stress for Justin, who had always worked on the premise that it was more

efficient if any shape currently in use carried at least two designs. Both Pansy and Oberon, Edwards had remarked, required a new look and some additional interest. Oberon was still by far Moorcroft's best-selling range. First it had toppled Cluny from its perch near the top of Moorcroft's sales league. Shortly afterwards it soared ahead of the Anemone Blue range, a design still in production after more than sixty years and one which until that moment had been the virtual Moorcroft trademark.

As part of a longer term project, Trevor had been set to work to produce a 9" and a 12" vase in the successful 80 shape. John was particularly fond of the 80 shape, and Trevor's first attempt at a larger model had resulted in a piece with an unacceptably thick neck. Little, in terms of shape deviation, passed John's eye unnoticed. The profile of the piece was wrong, and Trevor had been asked to refine the neck to emphasise the elegance of the piece. Rachel had plans for the 80 shape during the centenary year. Ideas began to form in her mind about poppies and the legendary bird, Phoenix. The elegant 80 shape featured in at least one of those ideas. Not surprisingly, activity in the mould-making shop during May and June 1995 was intense.

While Trevor Critchlow continued to extend Moorcroft's library of available shapes, Gill was putting the finishing touches to her plans for the 1995 Open Weekend. During early April Gill had been disappointed that a Bleeding Heart design by Rachel had been roundly rejected by both Hugh and her own husband, although the substitute

King Lear (1994, top) and
Cymbeline (1995) ginger jars:
Height 6"

FACING: *New shapes introduced between 1993 and 1997*
excluding the designer's Phoenix Bird piece

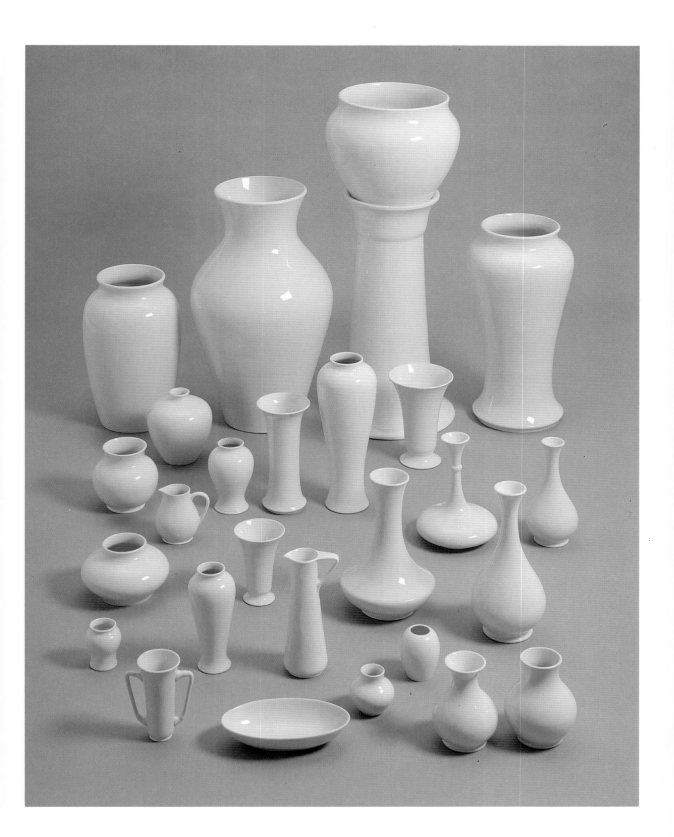

Hellebore was simple, pleasing to the eye and designed to one of her favourite shapes, the 102/5″. More significant for Gill was the fact that the municipal park behind the Works (formerly Cobridge railway station which had brought William Moorcroft to work in the early years of the century) had been incessantly occupied by travelling people during the previous year, and a distraught Stoke City Council had dumped ten tons of dirt and rubble at the entrance to prevent further trespass.

In the past, her collectors had used the park as a place to leave their cars during the Open Days, safely out of the clutches of traffic wardens and the local police. The heap of dirt was a disaster, and Gill set about making it quite clear that her collectors would never drive their cars over or around ten tons of Stoke-on-Trent rubble. The City Engineer was advised of the fact in short order, and after some gentle cajoling he relented. The municipal concession was, however, on the fundamental condition that the dirt mountain would be replaced first thing on the following Monday morning. Gill was triumphant.

A second success followed when Moorcroft Pottery's old friend from Canada, David Simmons, was persuaded to give the second Open Weekend lecture to collectors. The well-known broadcaster, John Sandon, an expert on Worcester porcelain, had already agreed to give the principal lecture some weeks earlier. Everything had been planned down to the last small detail, and whichever way Gill looked the arrangements appeared to be in order. For 1995 there were more trials available than hitherto, largely because of some extensive colour experiments conducted by Rachel and Wendy. The final touch was added by that family of very special people in the Moorcroft decorating shop who grafted their own artistic contribution onto the Open Weekend presentation.

As in the previous year, they had formed themselves into teams, each selecting a designer and tube-liner. Once the design had been completed, the tube-liner would apply her art to all team pieces, after which each decorator would individually colour a vase in her own preferred colourway. The general consensus at the Works was that the pieces on offer for auction were all even better than their predecessors in previous years, and excitement had begun to mount well before Open Weekend arrived. The auction was set out for preview in the Works' refurbished and redecorated packing house. As soon as John Sandon and David Simmons had finished their lectures at Stoke-on-Trent City Museum and Art Gallery, collectors were swarming around the tables examining not only the wealth of Rachel Bishop's trial pieces available but also the new designs especially drawn and decorated by the Moorcroft teams for the occasion.

FACING: *Hellebore Open Weekend vase 1995, height 5″; right Fruit mugs made for the Moorcroft Factory Shop in 1995 below left, Fruit vase trials, auctioned at Open Weekend 1995; right, Collectors' Club mug 1995*

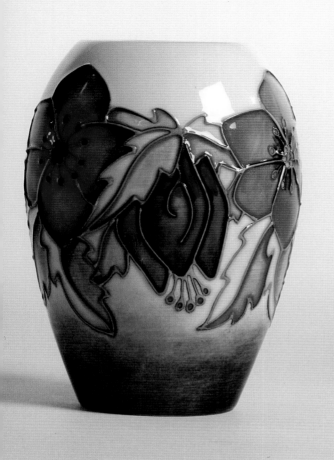

During the auction, on both Saturday and Sunday, the marquee's canvas flapped noisily in a strong, cold June wind. The bidding was a generous mixture of serious competition and good humour, most collectors having identified a favoured piece or two before auctioneer, Peter Blood, began accepting bids. It soon became clear that Justin Emery's experimentation into red glazes was moving in the right direction, if the prices achieved for the pieces on offer were anything to go by. Equally popular were some Rachel Bishop trial fruit designs, where three small vases notched up prices between two and three hundred pounds each.

It was, however, the Moorcroft decorators' pieces which once again proved the stars of the show on both days. On Sunday, Debbie Hancock's 'Indulgence', Hayley Mitchell and Marjorie Hill's 'Courtesan', Barbara Mountford and Shirley Hayes' 'Rainbow Tropics', and Sandra Eaton's 'Flora Rosa' (designer: Catherine Smith) all secured final bids in excess of five hundred pounds. The highest prices were achieved by Beverley Wilkes' 'The Harbour'. The piece she painted herself fetched seven hundred pounds on Sunday, while Sharon Austin's contribution was hammered down at seven hundred and ten pounds on the same day. Edwards had noticed for some time that there was a definite resurgence of interest in landscape designs, a phenomenon which became more pronounced each year. Beverley Wilkes' portrayal of a harbour scene was exceptionally well-proportioned, carried accurate design lines and a lively and varied colour combination.

For the weekend, collectors had been given the opportunity to purchase an attractive mug designed by Rachel Bishop and decorated with delicate flowers with the added option of having it inscribed with words of their choosing. One or two people were happy enough to take a mug without an inscription, but in the end only 60 were made. Additionally, Rachel Bishop's little Hellebore vase sold vigorously and by the time the last collector left for home on Sunday evening, all 160 pieces on offer had been sold.

Open Weekend 1995. 'Courtesan', a 12" vase by Marjorie Hill and 'Indulgence', a 10" bowl by Debbie Hancock.

SEVENTEEN

Phoenix Flies In

The summer of 1995 was both hotter and drier than anyone at Moorcroft could remember. During the June Wakes Holiday the old roof over the decorating shop had been dismantled, and in its place a modern roof appeared with a specification designed to conserve heat within the building during the winter months. The new roof brought with it an added benefit. During the blisteringly hot August days, the Moorcroft decorators soon noticed that the modern specification also kept out excess summer heat. The high pitch and Justin's specific instruction to the architects to incorporate ventilators had both combined to improve working conditions immeasurably. Additionally, it became a matter of pride for the Works Manager to look at the new floor in the decorating shop. Laid at a slight angle as before, the new smooth surface made hosing down and work hygiene much easier to maintain. In the end, it was the internal brick 'skin' constructed against the west-facing external wall that gave the most satisfaction. The double layer of bricks would keep out not only the cold, but also heat from the relentless August sun which in years gone by had seemed to burn its way through the original single layer of brick into the decorating shop.

Knowledgeable visitors walking round the decorating shop at the time would have noticed an odd vase or two decorated with poppies. A July design meeting at the Works had been shown a new Rachel Bishop Poppy vase which included, for the first time in decades, the Moorcroft 80/12″ shape. The vase, designed as one of the principal vases in the range, carried with it not only perfect proportions but also a subtle design which incorporated grey, green and orange shading almost to red. For John, who had pushed hard to reintroduce the shape, the sight of the first trial carrying a Poppy design, was an exciting moment. Consolidating her success earlier in the year with the Daffodil vase, Rachel's experiment in Poppy design had centred on the old Moorcroft technique of framing the principal image of the design with one of its secondary elements.

Rich orange petals of the poppies and dark stamenal centres of the flowers together created a combination of vibrant colour. Each flower had itself been framed with the grey leaves of the poppy plant, and even though the piece had a dark blue ground colour, the overall sensation was soft, generous and warm. The trial vase reduced the design meeting, usually a noisy affair, to virtual silence. John was the first to speak, and his comments, reflective as always, surprised those present. Poppies should be reserved for 1997. They should constitute a centenary range – no more, no less. John, of course, would have been the first to admit that he had cheated slightly. During its passage through the decorating process he had seen the poppy trial and studied it carefully. The Edwards made clear their preference not to be rushed into a decision, and the meeting agreed to adjourn discussion on the Poppy vase, which would be taken as the final item on the day's agenda.

The Moorcroft Board's decision to launch a new range based on the line and style of Charles Rennie Mackintosh at the Autumn Fair at Birmingham in September had been piecemeal by any definition. Hugh Edwards' love of Mackintosh's work had persisted for almost thirty years, starting with the aquisition of one of the few remaining watercolours by the great Scottish architect still in private hands. The painting, executed by Mackintosh at Warblerswick in 1914, had been given to his parents as a Silver Wedding present. Significantly, the spell it cast had lingered on. Every line on the picture reduced the flower, larkspur, to its purest essence.

Generally speaking, Mackintosh never wasted or misplaced a line, something essential in Moorcroft's own designs if the art of the tube-liner was to be used to the full. Sales Manager Steven Swann had reminded Edwards of the retrospective exhibition of Mackintosh's work to be launched in April 1996 in the architect's home city of Glasgow. Thereafter the exhibition would travel to New York, Chicago and Los Angeles, and the idea of a range designed in the Mackintosh style had been born at that moment. Trials for Moorcroft's tribute to Charles Rennie Mackintosh were produced spasmodically over a period of some months, but the range as yet showed no sign of coming together as a composite whole.

Rachel had made an extended trip to Glasgow to research original material, but the architectural structure of Mackintosh's work made the mood of his design intensely difficult to capture. Because Mackintosh, the architect, designed line by line with a vengeance, a single line drawn out of place would cause the whole design to collapse, just like a badly designed building. Rachel has a strong and stubborn nature, and refreshed by her holiday in Southern Ireland after her

FACING: *Poppy vase: Height 27"*

wedding, she set to work in earnest. By the end of August, the extent of the range had been identified and some trials were ready for approval.

The process of design approval at Moorcroft brings with it a huge temptation on the part of those present to say 'yes' to the very first pieces put forward for comment. An enthusiast, and both the Edwards and the Moorcrofts are enthusiasts, nearly always reacts positively to almost every new piece of Moorcroft the designer produces. This startling proposition will be easily understood by a serious Moorcroft collector, who can sense excitement at the sight of a new pot in whatever environment it is found. The knack for those making decisions is to balance that excitement with a cold appraisal of the design, both in artistic terms and as a production model.

The design road is strewn with the corpses of ineffective designers who have created the most wonderful design images but who, in the end, have been unable to deliver the reality of that design to those most important of all people, their customers. The price of this particular brand of failure is bankruptcy. Until a design possesses the attributes that can make it a reality, it is best to leave it as an optimist's dream. Great designs attain reality without destroying the dream which inspired them in the first place. For these reasons, only slight modifications to the Mackintosh vases were recommended.

Rachel had mastered Mackintosh's use of line. By changing the tube-lining from black to blue the Moorcroft designer was able to ensure that the mazarine blue featured at the top of the pot flowed right down to the base while a heather-coloured wash over undecorated parts of the pots was abandoned in favour of the pure ivory colour of the clay. After minimum debate Rachel and Justin were given the 'go ahead' for production, and Moorcroft prepared itself to launch the design

Designs taken from the Moorcroft Tribute to Charles Rennie Mackintosh

FACING: *Mackintosh lamp which won the Gold Award for Excellence against strong international competition at the Earl's Court Light Show in January 1996*

scheduled for the Autumn Fair at Birmingham in September. Steven Swann had pointed out to John that the standard Moorcroft lampshades were a hopeless misfit, and that the lamps would be more difficult to sell as a result. Rachel was quick to identify herself with the salesman's comment and designed new shades especially for the Mackintosh lamps, which John arranged to have made. Shortly thereafter that indefinable pre-launch tension surrounding any new design soon became a feature of daily routine at the Works.

It had taken a good deal of effort on Maureen's part to acquire two reproduction chairs based on Mackintosh's Argyll Tearoom design in time for the Birmingham Trade fair in September 1995. From her own home she took an Arts and Crafts table made in 1904 and using the chairs and table as 'props' created a backdrop for the range which caused visitors to the trade show to stop dead in their tracks. Rachel and Steven added their own touch to the layout of the pots and lamps on the stand. In the past, the designer's input on a Moorcroft trade stand had been minimal, but with the team working in concert, a combination of artistic flair, good layout and some striking pieces of furniture produced the desired effect.

By the time John and Gill returned from a tour of New Zealand three weeks later, the Moorcroft sales team, with Maureen at its head, had sold more pots at Birmingham on the first day than they had sold during the whole show the previous year. More significantly, the team effort on the stand, managed as a low-cost event, caused the total value of orders to exceed the total achieved during a more extravagant Moorcroft presentation at Harrogate earlier in July. Maureen Edwards had been right. The pots sold themselves. Like the imitation Mackintosh chairs and the Arts and Crafts table, the people present were only 'props'. Moorcroft pottery had become generic, with sales depending solely on the quality of the pieces in both design terms and in terms of technical excellence, rather than by virtue of those who sold them or their place of sale.

Shortly after the launch of the Mackintosh range *The Glasgow Evening Times*, in an enthusiastic article, referred to Rachel as a 'prodigy'. At the Earls Court Light Show in January 1996, her 14″ lamp base designed as Moorcroft's Tribute to Charles Rennie Mackintosh secured the show's Gold Award for Excellence against competition which included the best in Europe. Rachel's design beat them all. For the first time Hugh had the courage to compare Moorcroft pottery today with pieces made during the early years of the century. The result of that comparison was a very surprised Rachel, who found herself on the receiving end of a spontaneous hug.

FACING: *Tree Bark Thief, detail*

Moorcroft designs based on the work of William Morris. Tree Bark Thief jardinière and stand (facing) and 14″ vase (top left).
Snakeshead, lamp base 12″ (top right). Strawberry Thief, rear vase 7″ (bottom left). Leicester, rear vase 8″ (bottom right):
Part of the William Morris centenary collection

A design prototype which had caught John's eye during one of his early morning walkabouts around the decorating shop used tube-lining to create a complex and very tactile image of a feather. Phoenix, Rachel had called it at the time. The piece had a delicacy in its maze of tube-lining which earlier Moorcroft designs using feathers had perhaps lacked, and a warmth which those who had seen it found appealing. The Phoenix design was presented at the July meeting for the Board's reaction to be gauged. Gill had reservations and said so. John liked it, and so did Maureen. Hugh, the man of words, said nothing.

Rachel's use of the name Phoenix, spontaneous as it was, had stirred something deep inside him. Just for a moment he saw his own time at Moorcroft in his mind's eye. Those years had been the Phoenix years, and he glanced at Rachel to signify his approval of the trial piece. Sometimes a good trial piece can create an impact which demands favourable response from the outset. Sometimes the impact of a trial piece can be much more fundamental for any number of emotional or personal reasons. With thoughts almost too complex to articulate, Hugh acknowledged that he was more than happy to go along with John's suggestion that 'Phoenix' should be introduced to the public in February 1997 at the Birmingham International Spring Fair rather than in the autumn of 1996 at Birmingham. Both the Lamia range and William Morris centenary collection would have been exposed to the market for twelve months, and two new ranges for the centenary year was a sensible move forward. Despite a few stifled mutterings from Gill, the Board agreed.

First Phoenix trial: Height 5"

The popularity of Golden Lily was in decline. Sales returns were uncompromising about that, but 1996 was still the William Morris centenary year. In his time William Moorcroft had been a great admirer of Morris. Among their family papers John and Gill had found an original handwritten eulogy by William Moorcroft on the lifetime achievements of Morris. The text had been published in the December 1991 Collectors' Newsletter, and from that time the tie between the two Williams had been firmly recognised by both Moorcroft enthusiasts and Morris enthusiasts alike.

Edwards already knew that Rachel was struggling with a massive jardinière and stand on which she had re-worked Morris' Tree Bark Thief design. Initial objections from Justin about the lack of 'practice pieces' for the jardinière and its stand were recognised and dealt with in a novel way. Rachel drew Tree Bark Thief to the 121/14" vase introduced that year for Daffodil and one of the pieces used to extend the Foxglove range. It was, Gill commented, the only time a fourteen inch Moorcroft vase had been chosen for practice purposes! The sheer size of the jardinière and stand left the Moorcroft Board with no other option than to limit the edition to fifty. The price tag would inevitably be high. If more than fifty pieces were made the production programme would be impossible to complete in time for 1997 to arrive unencumbered with 1996 limited edition hangovers.

It was John who suggested that Tree Bark Thief on the 14" vase should itself be made as a limited edition. Tree Bark Thief on a jardinière and stand as well as a quality vase would make a significant

Part of William Morris centenary collection. Golden Lily, tall vase 10"

contribution to the William Morris centenary presentation, but much more was required and Rachel knew it. Taking her authority from an earlier design meeting, she was ready to introduce her own personal initiative. From a mass of fluffy tissue paper in a battered cardboard box she produced three lovely trial pieces each bearing different Morris design interpretations.

Leicester, Snakeshead and Strawberry Thief (two thieves in one collection, Edwards quipped) provoked animated and protracted discussion, much of which centred on the as yet non-existent 1996 Moorcroft catalogue. The consensus was for a two or even three-page catalogue presentation which would embrace not only the Tree Bark Thief vase but also four pieces in each of the other three designs, one of which had to double as a lamp. A nostalgic afterthought was the decision to retain the Golden Lily design on its ivory ground and run it in four shapes like the others. Rachel was given approval to proceed with further trials, and what had seemed at first to be a potentially dull year for the William Morris centenary, was now looking distinctly interesting.

For Edwards, the design meeting was going well. If all design and experimental work were to be completed by June 1996, current activity had begun to look more like an exercise in tying up loose ends. From where she was sitting, Maureen could see an 8″ plate still protected by bubble wrap in Rachel's cardboard box, which she guessed was a 1996 year plate trial. In fact there were three, all of which provoked serious discussion. Rachel's chosen design was Morning Glory, and she glared fiercely at Edwards as soon as the name was mentioned. That look reminded him of the damp, miserable car park in Stratford-upon-Avon three years earlier and the trial Collectors' Club piece which Rachel had produced from a blanket in the boot of her car. Rachel's work had matured since then, and the year plate trials all had style and a depth of colour which made each of them very appealing. An improvement, Edwards had whispered in her ear! If the others heard, they would certainly not have understood the implications of the remark. It was best that it stayed that way.

Still missing was the 1996 Special Occasions vase, and until Rachel produced from her cardboard box a contemporary version of Noah's Ark on a 6″ ginger jar, so too was the 1996 Collectors' Club piece. Gill pounced. The design included a medley of endangered species, and it was, Gill announced, absolutely perfect for her collectors – apart, that was, from the turtle which (according to Gill) looked as if it was in flight. Rachel agreed to remove the turtle, leaving Gill with her triumphant smile. Edwards was not entirely sure about the vase. To put animals on

Morning Glory Year Plate 1996
Diameter 8″

a pot carried a risk that the piece would be considered slightly 'naff'. Collectors would always vote with their wallets, but it was not an issue which merited conflict. In many ways, the Noah's Ark ginger jar was a compromise and, significantly, Gill was happy.

The meeting's ill-considered decision on the second limited edition piece for 1996 was unfortunate, yet at the same time understandable. During the busy summer weeks, Rachel's design inspiration had been hurt by the pure mechanics of her job. New ranges, limited editions and modifications to existing ranges had made it necessary for the Moorcroft designer to prepare almost two hundred and fifty drawings from which the teams in the decorating shop would work and which were an essential part of Moorcroft's art.

John had gestured vaguely in the direction of a Bishop water colour of a charger in the Lamia style which hung on the office wall, and Rachel looked relieved. Only later that same week did Edwards strongly articulate serious dissent at the decision. The charger was irrefutably part of the Lamia story, and the 14″ Tree Bark Thief vase was irrefutably part of the William Morris presentation. His conclusion, admittedly deferred, was that to proceed with a second Lamia limited edition at the same time as a new Lamia range would be a mistake. Shortly thereafter John agreed, and the search for a new limited edition for 1996 looked set to continue.

Poppy had been relegated to the end of the day's design business, and very much because of the success of the earlier discussions a decision was difficult. It was, John had said slowly, asking too much of the Moorcroft work force, including

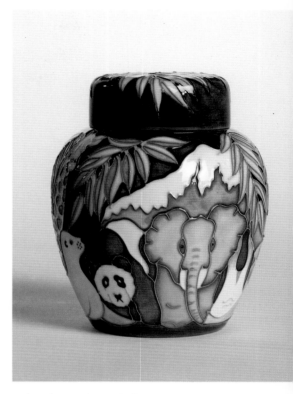

Noah's Ark ginger jar: Height 6″

Justin Emery, to expect them to produce the Lamia range, the William Morris collection and a new Poppy range in the same year, particularly if they had only recently come to terms with Moorcroft's Tribute to Charles Rennie Mackintosh. Additionally, Moorcroft had a bonus in the Phoenix pots, to be introduced in the centenary year. For that reason, he suggested, Poppies should wait until the centenary year at a time when the range would enjoy the full emotional appeal that the reintroduction of a poppy design would inevitably provoke. Edwards looked at his old friend and smiled. The comment was accurate, sensible and considerate, and Edwards was quick to identify himself with its wisdom. The two wives glanced at each other and followed suit. Poppy would be a Moorcroft centenary range.

EIGHTEEN

Ring out the Old

The dramatic success of the limited edition Lamia vase had made it inevitable that pressures would build up for a full range to follow. A number of collectors had remarked to Maureen during the Open Weekend following its launch that not everyone was rich enough to pay almost two thousand pounds for a single vase; even if they were, most had not moved quickly enough to secure a vase from their favoured retailer in response to Sean Slattery's emotive article in the December 1994 Newsletter. Happily for Rachel, Lamia fitted like a glove onto more than twenty shapes, and the problem for those attending a design meeting in August was more a question of what to exclude from the range than what to include. It was Maureen who suggested that a two-page catalogue presentation would be about right, and after animated discussion nineteen pieces were approved, including a clock and an elegant jug. For the first time, too, the 80/12″ appeared in a range. Although he had been the architect of the decision, John Moorcroft had been sorry to see the Poppy range postponed until 1997. Poppy included the 80/12″ shape, the re-arrival of which John had personally supervised during the preceding year. More significantly, the shapes selected for the Lamia range boasted no fewer than eight lamps, the fastest growing area of Moorcroft's art in a competitive but receptive market.

Edwards remained mute throughout most of that August meeting. His career in the law was fast coming to a conclusion, and he knew it. One of his favourite clients had recently formed a company called Bryony Investments Limited, a nice name Edwards had thought at the time and thoroughly wasted on a company. That simple fact encapsulated his problem. The world of the applied arts was calling more strongly than ever before, and this time, much as night followed day, his legal career was to be the loser.

One evening in September, he had arrived home late and tired. Maureen was waiting for him with an unexpected parcel which had arrived by courier from

FACING: *Tube-lining a 14″ Lamia vase*

Stoke-on-Trent a few hours earlier. The accompanying note from John advised that it contained five trials of 'Bryony', a design which Rachel had suggested as a possible Special Occasions vase for 1996. Neither Hugh nor his wife had ever mentioned the name 'Bryony' to Rachel, and the five trial pieces were all the more pleasurable to unwrap as a result. The Edwards' strong preference was for a prototype decorated on a green/yellow ground, and since this coincided with John and Gill's view, the design went forward for final trials with only one or two minor alterations.

The Bryony company and the Bryony vase stood together as Hugh's stark, personal choice. But thirty years in the law with Richards Butler was enough, and on 20 November 1995 he wrote his resignation letter to Senior Partner, Tim Archer. Under the terms of his partnership deed he was obliged to give not less than one year's notice in writing, and the exit date selected was 30 November 1996. Hugh calculated that this would give him a month to prepare for Christmas with his family, plus a little time to put in place the final touches to the Moorcroft centenary celebrations. Freedom from the constraints of his law practice would also enable him to spend more 'hands on' time at the Works and play his full part in the centenary events. His resignation letter caused something of a flutter in the law firm's dovecote, as Hugh had anticipated. It was quickly agreed that a press announcement would be postponed until a later date, and Edwards' role as head of the firm's Corporate and Com-

Bryony: 1996 Special Occasions vase. Height 5″

mercial Group and, as a senior member of the Richards Butler Board would both have to be carefully unravelled and his successors identified. For good measure, his loyal secretary Jo, who had married during the summer, announced that she was pregnant and would be leaving Richards Butler in June 1996. Edwards was delighted for her and said so.

Back at Cobridge, Walter Moorcroft was rumoured to be behaving in an odd way. He had requested and received a 'green' undecorated vase of the same shape and size as the Lamia limited edition vase and had carried it to an outhouse to work alone. Rumours began to percolate around the Works that a landscape design was in the course of preparation. If the rumours were true, Walter himself would have

FACING: *Pieces from the Lamia range: tallest vase from selection 14″ (bottom right)*

undergone his own personal revolution. Certainly he had agreed to design a piece for the centenary year, but never in his wildest dreams had Edwards considered the possibility that Walter would break the habit of a lifetime and draw a landscape vase.

It was Walter himself who put Edwards out of his misery. In the outhouse, the raw clay pot had been wrapped in wet newspaper and towels to keep it moist for the tube-liners. When Walter whisked the last damp tea-towel off the pot with a flourish that would have done credit to a magician, Edwards was confronted by a sight that no other collector had seen in the fifty years Walter had contributed his art to Moorcroft. The vase was not coloured or even tube-lined. All that could be seen was the purple outline of ink tracing, but the design was unmistakably that of a classic English landscape. While Edwards stared in utter disbelief, Walter talked of his ideas for colour, and as he did so it was as if the wet clay began to form colour before Hugh's eyes. The sky would be a mix of grey with strong sunlight shining down onto a hillside of fields and trees. The clouds would be grey and ominous to create a vivid contrast between light and shade on the countryside beneath, reflecting Walter's own perspectives on our vanishing meadows and woodland today and the ravages heaped upon nature in the name of progress.

Theoretically Walter had been retired for almost ten years, but if this was retirement Edwards' own anxieties began to fade. There were no words that he could muster to express his feelings. All that came out was a weak 'thank you' coupled with an expression of understanding of Walter's reasons for his historic change of heart. It was not a change of heart, Walter boomed. The world itself was changing; not his heart. The storm passed, and with a twinkle in his eye he asked whether the vase would appear as a limited edition. Edwards thought carefully. A landscape vase designed by Walter Moorcroft, one of the greatest potters of our time, would be a piece which collectors all over the world would greet with pleasure. It would be a sensational addition to Moorcroft's centenary presentation, and as such would proudly take its place at the International Spring Fair at Birmingham in February 1997. For that reason, and to emphasise its unique qualities, the vase would be produced as a limited edition of perhaps two hundred pieces. Hugh felt sure that the Board would agree.

Rachel's vision for the centenary year was something altogether different. The frenetic design activity during the summer had sapped her inspiration. Considerably disappointed, she had confided in Gill the personal implications of the Board's decision to abandon the Lamia charger as a limited edition in favour of an

FACING: *A landscape vase by Walter Moorcroft: 'After the Storm'*

unspecified 'something else'. Patiently Gill led Rachel through a series of possible options and ideas, but the spark of fresh inspiration failed to ignite. One after another flowers were dismissed. Photographs would not move her. They reflected someone else's art and not her own. Like the poets, her inspiration came as much from her emotion and state of mind as from images which she could see with her own eyes.

In the event, philosophical talk of love and beauty triggered a mention of the flower 'love in a mist'. The name struck a chord, and Rachel was able to refer back to an exceptionally stylish drawing of the flower which she had prepared nearly two years earlier – only to be told at the time to save it for a more auspicious occasion! For Gill, it was perhaps ironic that the end result was very much a Florian ware-style 'blue on blue' design with a hint of purple which gave the piece an almost 'Hesperian' appearance. Rachel had finished her colour combination with a touch of green, and the missing limited edition was missing no longer. The first trial, dated 18 October 1995, made Edwards smile. It was his wife's fiftieth birthday, and he was the first to admit that the vase had all the qualities of excellence last seen in Lamia. He also knew that the design, moving as it did from a blue colour base, was alien to Rachel's nature and all the more special as a result. That first trial vase, even though the neck is slightly out of line, takes pride of place in the Edwards' personal collection.

Love in a Mist: Height 12"

FACING: *Love in a Mist (detail)*

NINETEEN

Centenary: Trials and Tribulations

Edwards had just tidied up his desk. In front of him lay a dozen or more printed certificates representing seventy-three thousand, eight hundred and fifty-six shares in W. Moorcroft Plc. Sitting astride three of the certificates were the first prototypes of Rachel's Phoenix pots. One of them carried the image of the Phoenix bird as Rachel saw it in her mind's eye; the other a glorious fan of feathers. The irony was not lost on Edwards. Phoenix would be running as a small range in the centenary year. The Phoenix bird came from nowhere; the range had not been planned, but like so much at Moorcroft Phoenix had arrived notwithstanding. It had never been intended that Phoenix would represent Moorcroft's total recovery, but like the mythical bird that rose from the ashes the role was there to be played. The share certificates themselves did not look all that imposing, but together they represented sixty per cent of Moorcroft Pottery, and with that sixty per cent came a responsibility which at times Hugh almost preferred to ignore.

The early months of 1996 were very much a window of what was to follow during the remainder of the year. On the one hand pre-Birmingham orders soared to unprecedented levels, with sales of Lamia breaking all records before the International Spring Fair at Birmingham had even opened in early February. Close on the heels of Lamia came the William Morris centenary collection, while the value of orders received for Moorcroft's Tribute to Charles Rennie Mackintosh suggested that it might turn into a best-selling range. The implication of this huge surge in sales was not lost on Edwards. By the end of the first week in March, Moorcroft had 70% more orders on its books than it had had at the end of March the previous year. These

FACING: *Hugh Edwards with Phoenix pots.* RIGHT: *3" Phoenix pot and a Moorcroft peacock feather pot: c. 1900*

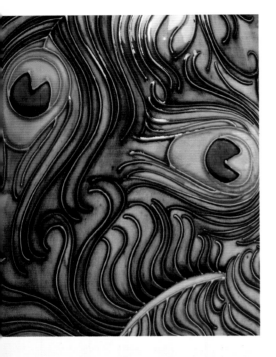

Pieces from the Phoenix range

figures excluded limited editions, all of which had sold out, and the special vases that Moorcroft would offer to collectors during 1996. Two months later the total sales figure was fast approaching the total value achieved during 1995. Somehow Justin Emery was still managing to cope and at the same time responded generously, if a little testily, to Rachel's requests for her programme of trials for the centenary year to be completed.

More than ever before, Justin had anticipated the increased demand. He had already taken steps to ensure that all seats in the decorating shop were filled, and had additionally set himself a target to complete Moorcroft's final training programmes before the end of the year. Even so, the production pressures on the Works Manager were enormous. Right through to June, Rachel's particular problem was to find a slot in the kiln firing processes to put through her remaining trials. Development of both Poppy and Phoenix were running in parallel. Shortly before the new three-day Open Weekend at the end of May, the Board decided to close the Phoenix range at nine pieces. Rachel suggested to Hugh that the range should include a 102/3″ vase. She knew that the profile of the vase had been taken from an old piece of Florian ware Hugh had found in a Parisian flea market about the time she had entered primary school; she also knew how pleased he would be to see the shape re-introduced, and in any event it suited her purpose.

Poppy was finally approved with no fewer than twenty pieces in the range, now including Rachel's first 27″ RM3 vase as the flagship. Justin's consumption of pills for his heart increased on the day that news of the RM3/27″ Poppy vase was announced. A trial of that magnitude was almost one push too far, but in the event he coped. Edwards decided to keep to himself details of a second 'green' RM3/27″ vase he had looked at with Rachel on which she had drawn cow parsley

FACING: *Pieces from the Phoenix range: tallest vase 14″*

and a laneside scene of wild flowers in late spring. Those were images of the future, destined to remain locked in the heads of those who had seen them for many months to come.

For Hugh it was an altogether curious state of affairs. At the beginning, he had put together piece by piece a collection of old Moorcroft which represented an almost complete history of the Pottery's past. Now Moorcroft was part of his life, and through the design process he had the capacity to see into Moorcroft's future and the pots still to come. These same pots would themselves one day become part of the company's rich history. It was not an unpleasant thought, but one which troubled him faintly. For years he had been accused by some of being a dreamer; others had actually encouraged what they called the 'vision thing'. But the truth was that unless he could continue to plan his way into the future, he became bored. For Edwards neither the world nor time ever stood still.

Poppy group: tallest vase 16″

From early January onwards, the task of carrying out centenary trials during Moorcroft's most hectic production period was a severe challenge to the fragile relationship between production and design. To ease the strain on both herself and Justin, Rachel retreated to her beloved Hampshire for extended periods of time to complete her art work, leaving the Works Manager to perform minor miracles in balancing the firing of her existing trials with his own training programme and delivery of orders. The Edwards and the Moorcrofts were ready to offer additional support to Rachel on her return, in the same way that Hugh gave it to Justin while she was away. They need not have worried. Justin was ready with a complete set of trial pieces. By Easter, Rachel was able to show the Board drawings for most outstanding designs, including some first thoughts on what she called her centenary 'Carousel'.

The possibility of a Carousel had been mooted on and off during the preceding year. The central feature was a 14″ charger carrying a mix of fruit and flowers, all of which had been used by Moorcroft designers at one time or another during the preceding ninety-nine years. The charger was extremely difficult both to design

FACING: *Poppy group: tall vase 12″*

Carousel 14″ charger

and make. Moorcroft's repertoire of colour was pushed far beyond any preceding parameters: the piece carried no fewer than fifteen 'colour builds'. In creating this design Rachel dragged Moorcroft from ceramic chemistry to virtual alchemy. Spinning away from the charger were four vases all using a combination of woodsmoke and jade as ground colours, a theme picked up from the charger itself. After only one trial, the 159/10″ vase was discarded. Rachel had used foxglove flowers picked out from a design detail on the charger, but the colours clashed badly and the overall appearance was too close to the current Foxglove range for her liking.

After that false start, she commissioned a pair of new shapes to combine with two Moorcroft 'old faithfuls': the 6″ ginger jar and the popular 32/5″ vase. In earlier Phoenix trials a small 62 shape vase had been used successfully, and Trevor Critchlow was persuaded to upgrade the size of the vase and make a new 11″ mould. To complete a set of three 80 shapes, a 9″ vase was also modelled for the Carousel to take a design which included gentle jasmine flowers. Edwards watched the development of the new 62/11″ vase with interest. He particularly liked one section of the charger which featured a mix of columbine, redcurrants, hellebore and passionflower. The design flowed beautifully onto the vase, and the use of blue tube-lining in the centre of the passionflower was particularly effective. Rachel also used blue tube-lining to create the tendrils of the jasmine plants on her new 80/9″ vase, achieving a striking impact in the process. A subtle use of green and yellow created a stylised design where leaves created the main structure, with the flowers only a secondary feature.

Perhaps the strongest vase in the centenary Carousel was the familiar Moorcroft ginger jar, where the ground colour was monochrome rather than 'washed'. To make the design work Rachel used daffodils, rosehips and primroses, with the leaves and flowers of the daffodils framing the rosehips and primroses. If the first three vases had style and strength, use of the 32/5″ shape for the fourth vase was pure inspiration. A woodsmoke ground at the base of the vase shaded into jade near the centre. For a child of the New Forest like Rachel, the wild strawberry and blackberries with their simple white flowers needed no introduction. The Moor-

FACING: *Carousel vase: Height 11″*

FACING: *Full centenary Carousel.*   ABOVE: *Details*

croft Board fell in love with the piece as soon as they saw it, and the centenary Carousel was complete. The rich mix of colours used on all five pieces are very much in the Rachel Bishop idiom. As the Carousel trials progressed over the following months they appeared to mature. The colours deepened, the designs developed a sharpness and clarity, and by mid-summer something very special indeed was ready for introduction to Moorcroft collectors.

Open Weekend 1996 saw Moorcroft's first three-day event. The William Morris centenary was in full swing, and Edwards was pleased to see Paul Atterbury in action again at Stoke-on-Trent's Museum and Art Gallery lecture theatre. Paul knew as much about Morris as he did about Moorcroft. In the past the link between Moorcroft and Morris had been obscure, but William Moorcroft's handwritten eulogy on Morris discovered among old family papers put an altogether different perspective on the connection between the two men. The eulogy could only have been written by a man who deeply admired and respected Morris, one who certainly knew a very great deal about his life's work. Atterbury cleverly wove together the fabric of Morris's life illustrating his talk with examples of Moorcroft's art and glimpses of the shadow of Morris behind it. A very thoughtful audience made their journey back to the Works to reappraise Rachel's own tribute to Morris in her adaptations of Strawberry Thief, Tree Bark Thief, Snakeshead, Leicester and Golden Lily.

Most of Moorcroft's guests that weekend had not expected the restoration and refurbishment of the factory shop. Gone were the wires and gas pipes; gone was the crumbling wall paint and the old trade stands which doubled as shop fittings. What collectors found was a combination of oak, brick and iron all overshadowed by the mighty bottle kiln. Shop Manager Kim Thompson had supervised the whole process with the architects and shop-fitters from start to finish. Hugh's own comments had been simple. Whatever was done to the fabric of the shop, there had to be complete synergy between the old and the new. Nestling in the rafters were modern light fittings designed to explode clear, clean light on the pottery displays beneath. When the contractors had finished their work, Kim and her team were able to enjoy a working environment which paid homage to the past but at the same time provided all the benefits of modern retailing. Edwards was

Collectors' Club jug
1997: Height 8″

stunned by the transformation, and the past images of leaking roofs, buckets of water and falling brick faded from his mind.

After a number of options had been discussed and most of them dismissed by Gill, Hugh and John decided that the second lecture for Collectors should be given by Edwards himself. The refurbishment of the factory shop suggested a theme. Decades ago, the Moorcroft building had been constructed to the very latest specification of quality. Edwards, the property man and the man of words, was well-qualified to sketch the history of the factory's development. John offered to help and the 1996 Open Weekend lecture programme was complete.

Back at the Works the auction of the decorators' pieces was dramatic and, happily for the Moorcroft staff, so too were the prices. As usual, Hugh found

'Fantasia', 9.5″ vase by Sue Pointon (left); 'Oriental Blossom', 10″ vase by Mary Etheridge (right)

himself among the collectors at the preview but in a detached frame of mind. It was as if he knew personally each piece he picked up. Hugh knew the decorators, their individual styles of working, and through the medium of that knowledge had developed an altogether different attitude to each piece. The pot became synonymous with the person who had designed and decorated it. It became alive with a story to tell all of its own. Nobody would have noticed the change in the way Hugh looked at the pieces on offer. Why should they? He had never designed a pot in his life, but the man of words could now see and understand much more in each piece he examined.

To promote the interests of the Moorcroft Collectors' Club, Rachel had suggested to Gill that dragonflies might play a central role in the design on the centenary Collector's Club piece. She was well aware that Gill would have loved a design involving frogs. Gill adored frogs but had come to accept, probably correctly, that another frog design, even on a coaster, was unlikely to pass through a design meeting. A design featuring dragonflies was a compromise. The charger, rejected by the Board as a limited edition in 1995 because of its close ties to the Lamia design, was still a very attractive piece of work, and Rachel had been as determined to use it as Edwards had been determined to reject it as a limited edition. The dragonflies were modified to suit the confines of an 8″ plate, and a candelabra of small pink flowers which Rachel had seen growing near a New Forest pond were drawn against a blue ground to add interest. A total lack of opposition from Gill at a design meeting in April, coupled with a broad smile at Edwards' discomfort, suggested that she was happy with the dragonflies.

Several weeks later potential production difficulties emerged. Justin recognised that Moorcroft would be carrying an excess of 8″ plates during the centenary year. To produce in parallel the Collectors' Club plate, the 1997 year plate and the final plate in a series of three made for Thaxted Guildhall Trustees featuring the town's magnificent Church would have been impossible. Against an assurance

that sales of the Thaxted Plate would cease before any material quantity of the Collectors' Club plates came on stream Justin relented, and Gill's Dragonfly plate was taken forward for further trials. The design was attractive; Rachel was satisfied. Colour, however, presented an altogether different problem for the Moorcroft designer. Whichever way she changed the colour combinations, shading or ground colour, the result failed to come up to her own high standards. Eight trials later, Rachel suggested to the Board that the 8″ plate decorated with dragonflies was 'a dog' and should be abandoned in favour of something new. Scarcely the moment for high design drama, the Board agreed.

The classical jug introduced for Moorcroft's Tribute to Charles Rennie Mackintosh and Lamia had been enthusiastically received by collectors throughout the British Isles, a number of whom had written to say how much they liked the piece. Free from the burdens of the abandoned drangonfly plate, Rachel took up the jug and designed some irises to its contours. Two trials were made. The first design used a mix of maroon irises and bluebells set against a green washed ground. The second jug was even more striking. It too had a maroon iris and buds with an ivory ground colour at the top shading to dark woodsmoke on the base. But the feature that stood out and made this trial exceptional was a second iris coloured purple, blue and yellow. Initially, Edwards had feared a dispute with the Moorcrofts over the merits of the two pieces. In the event, after an Easter telephone conversation between Hugh and Gill, the woodsmoke piece was approved subject to a slight design modification.

Above: Gill Moorcroft's Frog coaster; below: 6″ Ponga Fern vase

Few English collectors had been aware of Rachel's Fern vase on the 87/6″ shape, designed for a New Zealand promotion towards the end of 1995. Only a handful were available for the home market, and most of those were released during Moorcroft's 1996 Open Weekend at the end of May. Despite a high price tag, the few pieces available were snapped up by collectors. The original Fern vase had been commissioned by Tanfield Potter in an edition of one hundred and fifty pieces. A 'New Zealand' theme had been requested, and it was John who put forward the idea of a fern design. The result was a simple vase decorated with the New Zealand ponga fern – a name Rachel finds difficult to say without smiling. Ferns are difficult for tube-liners, but relatively straightforward

Convolvulus mug

for decorators. In a designer's mind that simple statement had significance. If the Moorcroft tube-liners could refine their art further, a design featuring a mature landscape with trees would challenge the decorators to the full. Images of the New Forest began to crystalize in her mind, and her thought processes moved forward into the future.

During a week's photography session with Michael Bruce in Putney High Street, London in February 1996, Rachel had stayed at the Edwards' house in Essex. On the second day she had shown them some proposals for her centenary year plate, including not only some drawings but also three plates displaying a colourful pheasant with a curly tail. Hugh had never seen a pheasant with a curly tail before, and Rachel had been less than pleased when he said so. What followed was unusual. Hugh, arch enemy of the word 'traditional', used it in connection with the 1997 year plate design.

Collectors had expectations; in the same way Christmas cards came with Christmas, so tradition had to mark the centenary year. Edwards had no idea what 'tradition' might mean in this context, and the problem was tossed across to Rachel to unravel. Her solution was striking. It is an obvious truth that Moorcroft pottery first appeared in 1897 from the art pottery department at James Macintyre & Co. Ltd., but today the image synonymous with the Moorcroft name is its historic bottle kiln. Although the bottle kiln was not built until 1919, Rachel decided to use it for her centenary year plate design. The prototype was bold and strong,

10" Centenary plate, made in an edition of 750 (top)
Rough Hawk's Beard (bottom)

just like the great kiln itself. Edwards loved the bottle kiln. It had been a great source of strength and inspiration back in 1986, and he was more than happy that it should be part of the company's centenary image on the 1997 plate.

At a spring sales meeting, John had been reminded that the centenary year would include a large number of special occasions for him to attend. At the same time it dawned on him that no designs had appeared for the traditional 7/5″ shape he liked to use in conjunction with his in-store promotions. The truth was that both he and everyone else on the Board had forgotten the Centenary Special Occasions vase altogether. Rachel had not. From her artist's case she produced an attractive watercolour featuring flowers which at first John had thought were dandelions. In his mind, dandelions were synonymous with Neville Pundole, the year plate dealer, for whom Sally Dennis had previously drawn two Dandelion limited edition vases.

John was not a dealer like Neville, he reminded Rachel unhappily, and dandelions were by no means his favourite flower. Out came Rachel's book on wild flowers. The 'dandelion' was not a dandelion at all but Rough Hawk's Beard, a native biennial of arable land, roadsides and waste places. Roadsides and waste places were not what John had in mind for vases on which he usually signed his name 'on glaze' for the purchaser – particularly during Moorcroft's prestigious centenary year. But a kind man to the end, John let it pass. The Rough Hawk's Beard vase was given formal approval after slight modification at a design meeting in May, just one day before Collectors' Open Weekend.

From the beginning of the year, Gill had been incessantly reminding Rachel that her Open Weekend pieces for May were still outstanding. Once more the Moorcroft designer had been obliged to squeeze the last ounce of her creative ability to produce a mug decorated with Convolvulus flowers on the base of which

Collectors could request their own written message. The Open Weekend vase was an altogether different problem. Occasionally something akin to folklore rears its head at Moorcroft, usually introduced by the word 'traditionally'. The word irritates Edwards intensely, and when John remarked that it was traditional for Moorcroft to produce vases on an ivory ground for Open Weekend, he nearly blew a fuse. In an unusual gesture of openness, Hugh acknowledged his conversation about 'tradition' with Rachel a few weeks earlier.

Moorcroft's hard-pressed Works Manager was almost certainly behind John's comment, and indeed Edwards could almost feel his hand on the remark itself. Justin was under extraordinary pressure, and Edwards was obliged to acknowledge the fact. Hugh had suggested to Rachel more than once that nothing should ever be regarded as traditional – a rule he himself admits he promptly broke to clear the way for the bottle kiln to appear on Moorcroft's centenary year plate. After discussion the Board was persuaded that Rachel should be free to develop her design for the Open Weekend piece without restriction on colour or form. Hugh already knew that the Moorcroft designer's own preference was for a piece with a coloured ground, and that she had a design in mind which would use the 65/6″ shape. The 65 shape was a cheerful baluster vase which always reminded Edwards of his own silhouette. Rachel had solemnly told Hugh that the flowers featured in her design had no name. Spiral buds and clinging foliage wrapped themselves around the vase. The design was naturalistic, not structured. John liked the washed blue ground; Maureen and Gill liked the yellow flowers, and Hugh had nothing but praise for the heart-shaped leaves which crept out of the stem of the plant, their two-toned colours adding much charm. Gill was happy for just as long as it took to approve the piece for production and called it 'Tansy'. Almost immediately afterwards clouds gathered.

Tansy (top) and Spring Flowers mug

Rudbeckia: Height 8″

The hectic design activity which had swamped Justin and exhausted Rachel masked the fact that Open Weekend pieces for the centenary year had been overlooked. When Gill reminded those present of the omission, Rachel stared at her in disbelief. For the next week, if Rachel was about the Works, nobody noticed her comings and goings. If they had, to have asked questions would have been little short of brutal. Ten days later Rachel telephoned Hugh in London. For once the man of words was uncertain what to say. Rachel was talking quietly, as if she had just woken from a deep sleep. The Open Weekend vase for the centenary year would be the 122/8″ shape on which she had drawn Rudbeckia flowers which looked like large daisies. Only the side view had been used in the design; there were no buds; the flower at the top of the vase was pale golden yellow and the flower near the base more strongly coloured. Once again the design was naturalistic, not stylised, and would be set against an ivory ground. Hugh said nothing, and the voice continued. Also for Open Weekend there would be a mug covered with spring flowers divided by long, slender leaves. The voice stopped, and for the first time in thirty years Hugh silently cursed the telephone and the one hundred and seventy-five miles between the voice and himself. His thanks sounded hollow; the voice disappeared.

Hugh was deeply concerned about Rachel. Massive design output had dimmed her vision and weakened her will to go on. Even so, she had shown enormous strength of purpose and had delivered everything, literally everything, on time and on her own. By completing two years' design work in one she had enabled Hugh to stay on course to achieve his own personal dream for Moorcroft pottery to reach its unprecedented one hundredth birthday. At the same time the Moorcroft designer, schooled in the secrets of the New Forest, had shown Hugh, almost intuitively, how to rely on others once more as well as himself. Despite all the pressure there had been no tantrums, few tears, and very little evidence of despair. By the close of the centenary year Rachel would be a Moorcroft star in her own right, and achieve international recognition as a result. That was to be her reward, and Hugh looked forward to the day when she would carry the Moorcroft banner for the connoisseurs of the applied arts to see. The young woman who had shown him her interview portfolio at the end of 1992 had come a very long way indeed. Hugh was proud of her, and grateful too.

The Moorcroft banner would be a heavy burden to carry, but Rachel had already shown herself capable of dealing with the press, radio and television. The thought of her growing popularity with Moorcroft collectors and retailers alike had lingered on in Edwards' mind. By June his vision for the future was clear, and he called a management meeting to discuss Moorcroft's plans for the centenary celebrations. One of the proposals put forward was simple and to the point. Rachel would take her own design promotions to Moorcroft retailers and to exhibitions. To strengthen the impact of her visit the Moorcroft designer would bring with her a special vase of her own.

In that instant the concept of the Moorcroft Designer meeting collectors in person and through the media burst into Edwards' mind. Her promotions would be in parallel to John's, and she would have the added incentive to design a piece for herself as well as a piece for John. In August 1996, Edwards watched the trials of the Designer's vase pass through their final stages with intense interest. Rachel had selected a new shape which had not been used by Moorcroft for many decades, and around its contours she had designed her own vision of the Phoenix bird. The pot would be the only one in production carrying the image of the Phoenix bird itself, and Hugh had no doubt whatever about the reaction of Moorcroft collectors to this unusual glimpse into Moorcroft's future.

To work behind the scenes, without praise or profile, had been the Edwards' chosen role during the ten critical Moorcroft years leading to 1997, now dubbed 'the Phoenix years'. Hugh had been surprised when in January 1996, Richard Dennis made contact to ask for a picture of the Edwards to be included in a new print-run of Paul Atterbury's book, *Moor-*

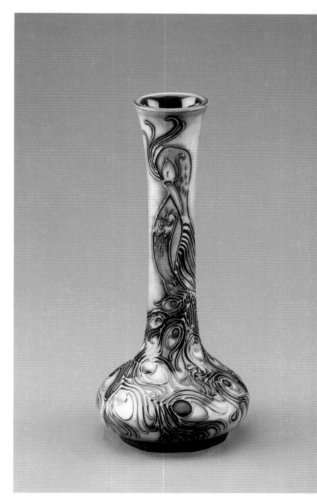

Designer's Phoenix bird vase: Height 8"

croft. He had been even more surprised a month earlier at Moorcroft's Annual General Meeting in December, when Alan Wright and his wife Rene had proposed him as Chairman of the company. John and Gill were quick to follow suit. It would no longer be possible for Edwards to quip to the Bank that he was the Accounts Clerk, or to embarrass the Auditors by saying that he was whatever they wanted him to be. If the truth were known, Edwards enjoyed working in the engine room of whatever ship he happened to sail in. He had little time for those who withered if they could not be photographed strutting the deck, who needed publicity to massage their egos or who believed that they were more significant than they really were.

One evening in September 1996, exactly ten years after he joined Moorcroft, Edwards found himself alone at the Works. The staff had all gone home. It was as if he could sense ghosts in the rafters, and there was a tingle in his spine as the last rays of light struggled to make their way through the large windows at the western end of the decorating shop. It had been a day of laughter, and a sensation of pure happiness engulfed him. That sensation had eluded him completely when he had first entered the building ten years before, but it now came mixed with thoughts of the past. In his mind's eye he could see the sweating men who stoked the great coal furnaces; William Moorcroft ruling his empire with a rod of iron, dressed in a smart suit and sporting a bowler hat; young Olive Leeke, the ware selector, collecting pots from the saggers, still warm from the kiln. Olive had retired from Moorcroft the previous Christmas, after more than fifty years with the company. For a moment he could hear the crash and clatter of machines and the whirring of the belt drive which powered the throwing wheels and turning lathes; the shouting of men and women in the clay shop; the eerie silence in the decorating shop where staff had been forbidden to speak all those decades ago; and the insidious, sulphurous smoke that seared into the furthest corners of their lungs – all had gone. Only the ghosts remained. Edwards shivered, switched on the alarms, locked the door and left the building. Ideas had already begun to form in his mind about Moorcroft's contribution to the millennium.

Pair of unfired 'green' pots showing images of the New Forest

Epilogue

It was a clear winter's night and a light wind blew gently over the East Anglian plains carrying with it that unmistakable iron cold of the Siberian mountains. The lights had been switched on in Thaxted church to invite all those who passed by to come inside and see in the new year. From the Swan Hotel immediately opposite could be heard the cheerful buzz of conversation between friends punctuated by the occasional outburst of laughter. Maureen was sharing a private joke or two with Thaxted people who had done so much to support her husband after he stood down as chairman of the Thaxted council more than ten years earlier to immerse himself in Moorcroft. Neville Pundole, Kim Thompson and her husband Chris were talking together with Debbie Colville by a log fire at the far end of the room. Alan Wright and Steven Swann were looking intensely at a small wood engraving of the Works which Rachel was holding. Steven would have travelled down from Stoke-on-Trent with the Thompsons that day, but Hugh had no idea where Rachel's journey had started. Graham Soal and his wife Margaret sat together. As Hugh's bank manager, it had been Graham who had first approved the availability of funds to invest in Moorcroft back in 1986. Everyone in the room had played a part in the Phoenix story and deserved a personal note of thanks. At five minutes to twelve, Hugh unobtrusively left the hotel with Maureen to walk across to Thaxted church. Others followed him including Rachel and the Wrights. He was conscious of that. The Thaxted Morris Men were inside, dancing to the sound of a traditional tune and each holding a 12″ Moorcroft 'Snakeshead' vase. The great church clock struck midnight. Simultaneously, the Thaxted bells pealed their message of joy at the arrival of the new year across the open countryside. It was 1997, and the first pots to carry the Moorcroft name were one hundred years old.

FACING: *The third in a series of three plates commissioned by Thaxted Guildhall Trustees and showing Thaxted Church. Diameter 8″*

Moorcroft Marks

TUBE-LINERS MARKS

Shirley Lowndes 1955–95	Marie Penkethman 1990 to present
Gillian Powell (Edge) 1977 to present	Catherine Beech (Smith) 1992 to present
Gillian Leese (Johnson) 1985 to present	Julie Auden 1993 to present
Ailie Woodhead 1987 to present	Joyce Keeling 1973 to present
Alison Neale 1988 to present	Andrew McMinn 1993 – 95
Katherine Keeling 1988 – 89	Amanda Bourne (Tarrant) 1994 to present
Karen Gibson (Potts) 1989 to present	Hayley Grocott-Smith 1995 to present

PAINTRESSES MARKS

Lily Gwynne
1945 – 54; 1956 – 60; 1989 – 91

Wendy Mason
1979 to present

Adrienne Wain
1947 – 64; 1987 – 92

Julie Dolan
1980 to present

Gwyneth Hibbitt

Lynn Ford
1984-88

Barbara Mountford
1958 – 66; 1987 to present

Hayley Mitchell (Moore)
1987 to present

Sue Gibbs
1961 – 75; 1984 to present

Jayne Hancock
1987 to present

Mary Etheridge
1961 – 68; 1987 to present

Jennifer James
1987 to present

Margaret Nash
1968 –91

Sandra Eaton
1987 to present

Sue Pointon
1970 – 79; 1988 to present

Sharon Austin
1987 to present

Angela Scoffins
1974 – 92

Mandy Dobson
1987 to present

Christine Brundrett
1977 – 89

Marjorie Hill
1987 to present

Hayley Smith 1988 to present		Debra Hancock 1992 – 93	
Jackie Moores (Degg) 1988 – 1995		Shirley Anderson (Hayes) 1992 to present	
Katherine Lloyd 1988 – 92		Sally Anne Bailey 1992 – 93	
Julie Rushton 1988 to present		Susan Gwyneth Clarke 1992 – 93	
Beverly Wilkes 1989 to present		Elizabeth Smith 1992 to present	
Janet Kirkland 1989 to present		Lorraine Knowles 1992 to present	
Paula Nixon 1990 to present		Maggie Thompson 1992 to present	
Sylvia Abell (Evans) 1991 to present		Julie Shenton 1993 – 94	
Lisa Phillips 1991 to present		Joanne Mountford 1994 to present	
Jackie Norcup (Rowe)		Emma Rafferty 1994 to present	
Sian Leeper 1992 – 93		Mandy Wood 1994 to present	

Joanne Morton
1994 to present

Sarah Wallis
1995 – 96

Amanda Baggley
1995 to present

Susan Barnsley
1995 to present

Stella Dawson
1995 to present

Angela Davenport
1995 to present

Karen Mellor
1995 to present

RETAILER AND DISTRIBUTOR MARKS 1993-1996

Ponga Fern vase made exclusively for Tanfield Potter, New Zealand.

6″ Ginger Jar made exclusively for B & W Thornton. "Cymbeline" - last in a series of five limited edtions of 250 each based on Shakesperian themes. All have the same retailer marks

The Sulpher Crested Cockatoo design made as a 10″ vase and plate in an edition of 60 and 350 respectively for Moorcroft's Australian distributor, Philip Allen, did not carry a special distributor's mark.

The Windsor Carnation: the vase (an example of which was presented to H.M. The Queen in 1996) was made exclusively for Talents of Windsor in an edition of 300 pieces.

'Malahide' a limited edition of 200 vases showing the Bottlebrush shrub. The edition was made exclusively for James Macintyre & Co Ltd, Victoria Quarter, Leeds. (Right)

YEAR STAMPS 1990-1997

1990	← ◄◄◄	Arrow	1994	Eye symbol	Eye
1991	Bell symbol	Bell	1995	Flag symbol	Flag
1992	Candle symbol	Candle	1996	Gate symbol	Gate
1993	Diamond symbol	Diamond	1997	H symbol	Centenary Mark (H & C for Roman hundred)

SPECIAL MARKS

Painted mark MCC + Year denotes a piece made and sold on Moorcroft's Open

Weekends each year. Marks for 1993, 1994 and 1995 shown.

Index